THE DEMONIC AND THE DIVINE

THE
DEMONIC

and the

Divine

DANIEL DAY WILLIAMS
Edited by Stacy A. Evans

FORTRESS PRESS   Minneapolis

THE DEMONIC AND THE DIVINE

Cover design: Carol Evans-Smith

Internal design: Karen Buck

Library of Congress Cataloging-in-Publication Data
Williams, Daniel Day, 1910-1973.
   The demonic and the divine / Daniel Day Williams ; edited by Stacy A. Evans.
   p.   cm.
   Includes bibliographical references.
   ISBN 0-8006-2431-9
   1. Demonology. 2. Good and evil. 3. Theodicy. 4. Eschatology.
  5. Process theology. I. Evans, Stacy A., 1947-   II. Title.
BT975.W53 1990
235'.4—dc20
                      90-35602
                      CIP

The paper used in this publication meets the minimum requirements of American National Standard for Information Sciences—Permanence of Paper for Printed Library Materials, ANSI Z329.48-1984. ∞™

Manufactured in the U.S.A.   1-2431

94   93   92   91   90   1   2   3   4   5   6   7   8   9   10

*To the living memory of
Daniel Day Williams and
to the person who has
always believed in the value
of Dan's work, his wife,
Eulalia Westberg Williams*

Contents

Editor's Preface

The problem of evil and its effects has daunted humans since the dawn of civilization. Christians, like others, have experienced evil and its power and pondered their significance. Over the centuries Christian writers have wrestled with the existence, evident power, and pervasive qualities of evil and God's relation to it. Some have even written of the triumph of evil as the close of human history.

This volume presents the sustained reflection of a major American theologian, the late Daniel Day Williams, on this profound and enigmatic topic. Beginning with the idea of demonic power, he ranges over the topics of loss, tragedy, structural evil, death, immortality, and the end of all things to discern our part and God's involvement in the evil that plagues existence. Staying close to human experience and drawing on insights from the New Testament, depth psychology, and other theologians, Williams forges a clear and distinctive position of his own.

Part One, in which Williams deals with evil as it expresses itself in the power of the demonic, is based on lectures that he delivered in the Armstrong Lecture series at Kalamazoo College in Michigan in October 1973.

Part Two contains Williams's views on eschatology, the consideration of the end of all things in this world. He deals with this treacherous subject carefully and sensitively and focuses on both the individual and the world as a whole. These chapters contain Williams's thought as it developed over the last twenty years of his life. Throughout he emphasizes that love is the basic category in Christian theology. Because God's love is always available, Williams looks to the end of time not with dread but with hope.

Williams's treatment of these two areas is insightful, original, and not terrifying. He argues for the reality of evil and its forces, and he does not doubt that there will be a final chapter in human history. But his final assertion is that God will triumph regardless of circumstances and that, above all, God's goodness will prevail. Williams's deep engagement with process thought allowed him to approach such terms as *demons, last judgment,* and traditional Christian theological categories with a fresh perspective.

This volume appears seventeen years after Daniel Day Williams's untimely death at the age of 63. Yet the thought of this "senior statesman"[1] of process theology may perhaps be even more relevant as we approach the end of Christianity's second millennium. Those who know Williams's work will appreciate anew the courage of this Christian thinker, the compassion that informed his scholarship, and the pastoral character of his teaching style. A new generation will find here a caring Christian theologian whose work deservedly lives on.

—*Stacy A. Evans*

Acknowledgments

In the years since Williams's death, a number of persons have worked on the papers from which the present volume comes. The editorial skills and loving attention of Penelope Washbourn, Lee Snook, Jerry McCoy, Jean Lambert, and Tony Wolfe have made the task of the current editor much easier and are acknowledged with deep gratitude. Without their work much of what this volume offers would probably have been lost. They realized, along with John B. Cobb, Jr., David R. Griffin, and others of the Center for Process Studies in Claremont, California (where the Williams papers are housed), that the long-range contribution of Daniel Day Williams should not be stymied by his untimely death. I thank those named and others at the Center for Process Studies and at the School of Theology at Claremont for their support and helpfulness during preparation of this book. I thank Susan Malone for retyping the manuscript before submission to the publisher. Also, I thank Eulalia Williams, Dr. Williams's widow, for her assistance and keen interest in this project, and for her personal kindness. I am grateful to the staff of Fortress Press, especially J. Michael West and Stefanie Ormsby Cox, and to Sheryl Strauss, for their timely suggestions and support in helping these writings be published. I thank the leadership of Broad Street United Methodist Church, Columbus, Ohio, who gave me the time during the summer of 1987 to work on this project while I was pastor there. Lastly I acknowledge with deep gratitude my wife, Cheryl, and my family for their moral support and understanding during the time away from them during preparation of the manuscript.

PART ONE

The Clash
of the Demonic
and the Divine

1

Faces of the Demonic

In 1940, Dr. Paul Tillich gave lectures at the University of Chicago arguing that the category of the demonic is important in the interpretation of history.[1] He had already experienced the fanatical and destructive powers set loose in the Nazi regime. World War II had begun, and although the world was then far from knowing the full horror of what was coming, we were beginning to seek symbols profound enough to express the depths of the abyss toward which civilization was moving.

In recent years "the demonic" has been developing in our language as a category, as a symbol of evil, and as a significant religious concern. We see, for example, the phenomenon of revivals of cults of satanic worship and witchcraft. This is not my central concern in this discussion, although the pathological fringes of society are symptomatic of the widespread fears that produce interest in the occult and morbidly bizarre.

We can recognize the reality of demonic modes of experience and forms of power without committing ourselves to belief in demons as supernatural beings flying about the world at the command of an archfiend, one of whose names is Satan. Rather, we are seeking to understand the demonic as an experienced mode of action; it enters our human history with describable effects. These are so fundamental that a major theme of religion has been the conflict with demons, and a secular analysis of social forces requires the concept of the demonic. In our time, in fact, literature and the other arts are probing the demonic realities in experience just as profoundly as is theology. "The brave play of language at the brink of inexpressible horror is what the age demands."[2]

3

The necessity of this category for understanding human existence is therefore not a private concern of religious thought. The demonic is the dominant motif of the most sensitive artists in our culture. From Franz Kafka to Kurt Vonnegut and Thomas Pynchon, and from Fyodor Dostoyevsky to Edward Albee and Samuel Beckett, those who probe most deeply have portrayed the mystery of a kind of evil that erupts with destructive fury. Auschwitz and My Lai are facts of experience in our history that take us to the ultimate depth.

Already we seem to be identifying the demonic as a form of evil. In the history of religions the story is more complicated. Demons are found first as special heavenly beings associated with the divine realm. In the early religion of Israel they are messengers of God with special functions; Satan first appears in the Hebrew Bible as an angel who serves God, sometimes in rather extraordinary ways. For example, he is the disturber of Job's peace: "Does Job fear God for nought?" (Job 1:9). Slowly a transition takes place, separating the heavenly beings into the good and the evil ones. In the New Testament the demons are wholly evil. They are under the command of Satan, the prince of demons. He is the supreme adversary who tempts the Christ and who wars against God and humanity to the end. Satan is a fallen angel whose initial rebellion has taken place in heaven. The prologue to human history is the war in heaven.

I refer to this tradition of the demons as known in religion in order to point out that the theme of the demonic and divine powers takes us to the central questions about the sources and relationships of good and evil, and therefore to the question of what we can hope for. Religion itself can be captured by demonic powers.

The historical approach to the meaning of the demonic would be highly instructive, but I propose here to take another, the phenomenological approach. Our first task is to describe as accurately as possible the forms of behavior in persons and in societies that can be designated "demonic." The word has been somewhat damaged by its frequent use to mean anything that we don't like or that troubles us, and especially by our applying it indiscriminately to our opposition. Not all evil is demonic. We need a clarification of this category, lest we fail to recognize its distinctive character and depth. Through a description of its special structure we may gain a clearer understanding of how the demonic power may be broken.

Tillich's Phenomenology of
the Demonic

Paul Tillich's Chicago lectures, to which I have referred, were in part taken from his essay on the demonic in *The Interpretation of History*.[3] What he says there is so important that I would like to review its main points as the first step in our exploration. The demons are not beings, Tillich makes clear; they are structures within being, manifest in experience, and they bear a special relationship to the ultimate reality that is the ground of all things.

In Tillich's doctrine, at the base of all reality is the meaning-giving, unconditioned power of being that is God's very self. The divine is positive, creating, fulfilling. But there is a depth in God, an abyss out of which freedom arises, and freedom gives power to threaten as well as to affirm meaning. God, the power of being, eternally fights against the threat of meaninglessness and overcomes it.

In human history this struggle is manifest under the conditions of finitude. The demonic is experienced as the meaning-destroying eruption of power that splits the personality and that fastens itself upon a society in such a way that freedom begins to be lost. The fulfillment of human existence is thwarted. This demonic reality is never sheer destruction; if it were it could gain no foothold in existence. It arises out of the depth of creative life. At one point Tillich defines the demonic as "the form-destroying eruption of the creative basis of things," but another statement in the same essay is truer to his intention: "The demonic is a union of form-destroying and form-creating strength." The demonic creates forms, symbols, liturgies, and political structures. Their demonic character is their drive toward systematic repression of meaning and freedom or toward chaotic self-destruction. Tillich reserves the term *satanic* for the symbol of absolute negation. He would agree with the philosopher Ernst Bloch:

> The satanic is the horror of total annihilation, of complete unsubstantiality, of seclusion fleeing to the definitive void in which it is secluded. The reality that has so far been at work contains plenty of such eruptions of original evil, but not yet its victory; once its victory were shown as definite and hypostatized, the religious space would fill up negatively, with a Prince of Darkness and demonic substances, as it had been filled up positively with God and angelic substances.[4]

Satan, therefore, is not a person. We personalize him as we participate in the demonic powers. He is the mask of the plunge toward annihilation.

Tillich follows this analysis with a complex study of the demonic in culture. For him, culture is always religious: that is, it has an ultimate concern at its core. The principal identifying mark of the demonic, in addition to its ambiguity in relation to creation and destruction, is its absolutizing of some finite realm as the bearer of all meaning. The demonic sanctifies as absolute a particular space, whether that be an economic system, a national state, or a religious institution. It is always exclusive in its claims to control life through some particular power in history. The demonic powers abuse the holiness of being by worship of local and limited deities that may or may not have religious names.

Notice Tillich's insight that the demonic attacks the lowest and highest levels of the person and culture at the same time. It exploits both animal craving and spiritual aspiration to produce the possessed state. Demon possession is the creation of the cleft personality through a disruption that pervades body and spirit. We see further that to find the demonic in social structures, we should look to the most sanctified and powerful forms of culture, not because sanctity and power are demonic in themselves, but because these are the forms through which the demonic invades. In Tillich's words, "not in chaos, but in the highest, most strongly symbolic forms of a time is the social demonry to be sought."[5]

We should not look for the demonic structures as something wholly external to us. We participate in them. In some measure we are possessed. We cannot make a neat separation of the divine from the demonic, but we see the clash of the divine and demonic as a warfare that pervades all our passions and commitments. In all our cherished ecstasies there lurks a threat to meaning and freedom. When traditional religions have said Satan is crafty, they have known what they were talking about, except that even they have usually underestimated the satanic subtlety.

For Tillich, breaking the power of the demonic can only be done by another power, the power of grace. The ecstasies that may destroy us can only be overcome by the ecstatic experience of a superior power. Human life and history move within this inescapable conflict. Tillich concludes: "There is only one certainty, that the demonic is overcome in eternity, that in eternity the demonic is depth of the divine and in unity with divine clarity."[6]

I shall criticize and depart from this doctrine of Tillich's, that the divine and demonic are ultimately one. But I accept the view that the demons have no power apart from their drawing upon the divine power.

Structures of Demonic Experience

Can we achieve a phenomenological account of the main aspects of the demonic reality? We need further clarification and must remain as close to concrete historical experience as possible. There is danger in assuming that we can make the demonic into an object. But, to turn the point around, unless we have some transcendence over demonic corruption we could not speak about it at all.

The phenomenologists tell us to concentrate on particular experiences, abstracting from them the structures that characterize them in order to achieve a precise grasp of what our experience reveals. I shall try to adopt that method now in speaking of five structures that are identifiable in certain modes of experience. Taken together they identify the demonic. They are faces the demonic wears.

The first is *fascination*. The demonic quickens interest and excitement. A dull or boring demon is not worth bothering about. The demonic possesses a mode of fascination that casts a spell over our attention, releases our passionate energies, and drives us beyond our will under the guise of fulfilling our freedom.

The ecstasy exploited by any compelling social group may furnish examples. In a published diary of a young girl who was engaged to a German storm trooper, the girl describes what it was like for German youth in the early days of National Socialism. In a passage too long to quote here, she describes a youth rally on the banks of the Rhine. It is the time of the spring equinox. She describes the eager crowds and says, "a desire began to burgeon within me, to be permitted to help, like these women and girls in the great work of our leader, Adolf Hitler. A torch had been thrown into my heart and it continued to flame and blaze. . . ." She speaks of being almost in a trance in the expectation of the evening rally. She describes the campfire, the marching tunes, the offering of the Deutsche prayer of thanksgiving, and then Hermann Goering's flaming address in his call to battle for Germany's freedom. "The rustle of the Rhine sounds like a prayer for redemption from foreign despotism." And then as Goering stood in the circle around the fire, she held a torch over his shoulder and the flame illuminated his face for all to see. She exults, "Who could have been happier than I?"

What is most sobering about that description is the overwhelming power of the experience. We realize that in such a situation we would not be able to avoid the spell without a power superior to our own.

True, many good and desirable experiences exercise fascination, but aspects characteristic of the demonic fascination can be uncovered. For one thing, there is its spatialism, the absolutizing of "our cause." The ecstasy is turned outward for the individual but inward for the group and nation. Others are "the enemy," "the foreign despots." It is a short step from here to crushing acts of violence against others.

A second structure of demonic experience is the *distortion of perception*. The demonic gains its power to shape, exploit, and ultimately destroy our personal being by causing us to see falsely. Later, set free from illusion, we may see we were taken in. This aspect of the confusion of our perception is critical for our analysis.

Plato's dialogue *The Phaedo,* in his account of the death of Socrates, offers an astute analysis of this process. When the soul is bound to its desires in this world it suffers the greatest of all evils. The evil is "that every soul when it is pleased or pained excessively is at the same time forced to take the source of this experience to be the very principle of clarity and truth." But the soul is deceived because these sources of pleasure and pain are visible objects. Our bodily perceptions absorb us and take us away from the truth. Here the Platonic view takes over: the mind, not the eyes, perceives what is really real; we may regard that as too simple an analysis, because the mind has its own illusions. But Plato has given us two vitally important points.

He has exposed the element of hallucination in the demonic seizure and, second, he has shown that this arises both from pleasure and from pain. Both that which deeply satisfies our senses, and that which makes us suffer and terrifies us, we take to be the "very pinnacle of clarity and truth." The demonic causes us to see in a distorted way by exploiting both desire and fear. Social and religious demonries keep the community suspended between promise and fear, between ecstatic satisfaction and threat of irretrievable loss, between heaven and hell.

Absolute claims, by their sheer pretension, can achieve a power of (autonomous) enforcement, unless some kind of distance can be preserved by freedom of critical reflection. Demonic fascination allows no standing back to question. One mark of a social demonry is its prohibition of freedom to criticize; if an individual or group were to overcome its complete enclosure by the pretension to power, the demonry might collapse totally. The demonic structure must forbid an independent standing place outside it.

At the same time that the demonic becomes this enclosing power, it has the characteristic of invading us from a source outside the self. This is the second Fall. We experience the demonic as a *seizure*. We are possessed, yet we internalize and accept this being possessed. If we do not fully accept it, a split tears at the root of the personality. If it is true that there is always a residual freedom so long as we are human, then the demonic will always produce an inner conflict. We are torn. The descriptions of exorcism often reflect this; the demons cry out in fury.

The union of desire and terror in the demonic experience may produce an ecstasy that feeds upon both. We know the fascination of violence and destruction. Freud discovered what he named the death-wish as a structure of the personality. The demonic powers draw upon this energy for the lure of destructive violence. So the demonic ecstasy compounds the will to power with the plunge toward chaos.

Because this can produce a cleft in the person and because it violates the deepest will—to power in unity with love—the demonic can produce both ecstatic response and radical repression of feeling. We do not pretend to understand the depth of cruelty of which human beings are capable; "hardness of heart" is a tame phrase for it. But analysis of the self, possessed by a power that invades the self from beyond, discloses the real depth of the abyss in spiritual existence. Cruelty is a compound of ecstasy and fear. This is why religions look for a power great enough to cast out the demons. The belief that this must be a power from beyond the self may be more realistic than humanism, which expects its overcoming through human effort alone. Alfred Weber's description of the experience in Europe between the two world wars is devastatingly clear:

> It was as if certain forces sprang up out of the ground; giants of action, crafty, hungry for power, which nobody had noticed before, seemed to shoot up like a crop of dragon's teeth. And a formerly unthinkable readiness was there in the bulk of the middle class on whose enthusiasm, one can well say, these forces were borne at the outset. An indefinable objective *something* broke loose that swept away values taken for granted and held to be unshakable, in a universal psychic wave. A collective, supra-personal force, chained and hidden till then, suddenly burst from captivity. Once it was out it was whipped up by every conceivable means and swamped, practically speaking, everything.[7]

We hear the emphasis on total inundation. Satan's promise is typical demonic language: "All [the kingdoms of the world] I will give you" (Matt. 4:9).

The third characteristic face of the demonic is *aggrandizement*. The demonic ecstasy feeds upon itself and demands more and more. This is partly because the demonic structure is swollen with the lust for power. Its craving is insatiable because it feeds upon its power of domination. Friedrich Nietzsche cries out, "There cannot be a God, because I could not stand it not to be him."

There is a fourth structure characteristic of demonic systems, especially social systems, that contributes to this pattern of aggrandizement. It is what I shall call the *inertia of established systems of control*. Something in the form of social order drives established systems to promote their own elaboration, seemingly as an inescapable natural fact. Systems of social procedure and control have their own momentum, which is exceedingly difficult to stop.

This is a common feature of our experience. Amusing but telling examples of this inertia appear from time to time, such as Parkinson's Law that work expands to fill the time available for its completion, and the Peter Principle that in a business or educational hierarchy each person rises to his or her level of incompetence.

I turn for another example to the realm of professional sport, specifically football. One of the sharpest critiques of our present phase of "spectatoritis" is given by Eugene Bianchi in a paper called "Pigskin Piety."[8] He argues that in contrast to religion as a free and hopeful form of play, big-time football is an extension of dehumanizing religion. It hampers the creativity and commitment of players and spectators by confining their energies to a tight circle of brutal encounters for profit and prestige. He develops this theme in an analysis of the ritual character of the game. For a few hours on Sunday afternoon, the world is confined to this experience, which has a beginning and an end, victory and defeat. In theological terms it has an eschatological structure with its own Armageddon: the Super Bowl. Bianchi also sees the college bowl games as the contemporary equivalent of fertility rites, celebrations of the renewal of life through "fertilizing the land with the seeds of competitive violence for the year ahead."

Bianchi's specific charges are that professional football (1) is based on the aim to injure, (2) has a completely authoritarian structure in ownership and coaching, (3) excessively values so-called masculine traits and relegates the feminine to a stylized prettiness on the sidelines, and (4) affects the spectators by taking them away from real life. It is the new opiate of the people. Football, he concludes, means the brutal domination of the weekly enemy for money's sake. "The wedding of violence and lucre throws a demonic aura around the gridiron ritual. The satanic implications of the rite carry over strongly into business, education, politics, and of course, international relations."

I believe Bianchi's picture is overdrawn, though in books by individual athletes we are beginning to hear from the inside the same story about the human cost of the game. I cite his discussion because it is a clear example of the principle of the inertial system. In order for the game to be played, people have to pay money to see it. They want not only the thrill of the sport but also the thrill of winning. Games must be won. Coaches must demand more and more of players and themselves, until the late Vince Lombardi could say: "Winning is not the most important thing. It is the only thing." Since there is a premium on physical size of players, injuries are greater. Star players demand higher salaries. New stadia have to be built at astronomical costs and they must be filled. One television- and refrigerator-equipped observation box in the Houston Astrodome costs a staggering sum to rent for a year. The point is that grown, intelligent people who love the thrill of the game, its beauty, its skill, and its spectacle are caught in a spiraling absorption of time, money, and spiritual energies out of all proportion to the significance of what is going on.

To keep the record straight, since I have cited Bianchi's article, I must disagree with what seems to be one of his presuppositions: that all practice of conflict and engagement in competitive struggle is dehumanizing and therefore demonic. I do not believe that is true. Combativeness, competition, the exercise of physical and mental strength and skill to test our abilities, even the love of winning, belong to our natural and creative equipment. They have their place in personal growth. Further, it is no more destructive on principle to watch a great athlete accomplish something we could not possibly emulate than it is to watch a great pianist or violinist exercise a discipline and technique we could not possibly achieve. The system becomes demonic when it leads to the destruction of persons and of the capacity to appreciate the enemy, when it blocks the participants' abilities to accept losing, to share the joyful celebration of the spirit of the contest, and to look for reconciliation at the end.

Since this inertial character of social and economic processes seems to be built into life, it may be mistaken to call the processes demonic in themselves. What we should say is that when the inertial character takes hold, it tends to corrupt the spirit. When we accept it without resistance, the demonic power is winning. It uses these inertial tendencies to gratify our craving for power and to exploit our fear of annihilation. We think, for example, of the inertial aspects of the arms race, where each nation seeks to have a more destructive weapon than the other. Because more destructive weaponry is more expensive, more and more of each nation's total economic system must be geared to arms. This is a fact of national existence that cannot be set aside. But particular interests use our fears to exploit the need for more arms out of all proportion to the fact. The forces that profit from the weapons business play upon fear. We may simply resign ourselves to the inevitable; but that is how the demonic power takes hold, diverting the spirit from its sense of justice and destroying the courage to resist exploitation.

I do not hold that the processes of nature and history are under the control of demonic powers. Yet, if one wanted to make a case for the doctrine of the fallen world lying under bondage to Satan, one might begin with the tendency to aggrandizement in the natural processes so that more and more of the possibilities of life are cut off by the need to preserve the systems that have been created.

We have touched upon the fifth characteristic of the structure of the demonic. This is its dimension of *ontological depth*. The demonic, we have said, erupts from beyond ourselves. We experience it as a revelation of power in the depth of things. The demonic is not experienced as merely a temporary phenomenon of certain kinds of human experience. It is experienced as a disclosure of depths that lead either to what is ultimately real or to utter annihilation. In either case, facing the demonic becomes a matter of ultimate concern about the decision between being and nonbeing. That is how even in a secular order the experience of the demonic raises the religious question, the final question about what it means to be in this finite existence and to be subject to the threats of life and death. Whether it is pursued philosophically or not, the question that underlies it is inescapable in human existence.

Because the question is inescapable, all secularisms produce a vacuum that will be filled with some kind of religiousness. A sober secularism with little ontological rootage is possible temporarily; at times it is even desirable, in order to give freedom from superstition and false forms of religion. But to be human is to want to know who we really are, and that question will be asked with existential passion in the encounter with the demonic realities. In his book *The Warriors,* a diary of his war experiences, J. Glenn Gray comments on the fury that sometimes possesses fighters:

> It is as if they are seized by a demon. . . . Anyone who has watched men on the battlefield at work with artillery, or looked into the eyes of veteran killers fresh from slaughter . . . finds it hard to escape the conclusion that there is a delight in destruction. A walk across any battlefield shortly after the guns have fallen silent is convincing enough. A sensitive person is sure to be oppressed by a spirit of evil there, a radical evil which suddenly makes the medieval images of hell and the thousand devils of that imagination believable. This evil appears to surpass human malice and to demand explanation in cosmological and religious terms.[9]

The experience of the demonic involves this disclosure of the depths of being. The awe that religion knows in the presence of creative power is also present here, now infused both with horror and with the frenzy and ecstasy of the destructive impulse. We see more clearly why the demons are fascinating. They reach the roots of our being. They fuse life and death in the heat of consuming passion.

Because the demonic structures in experience have this ontological dimension, I believe there can be no powerful resistance and response without the disclosure of the ontological depth of grace. The divine must become present with power. That is why a positivism, which remains on the surface of experience, is powerless in the face of the demonic.

We have identified some traits of the demonic structures, assuming that there is some way of discriminating between this form of destructive evil and the health and wholeness of the good. How do we know whether we are dealing with the demonic or with divine creativity? The answer has to be a pragmatic one. We can know only by discovering the consequences of human actions, and we must have a norm for assessing those consequences.

We are not completely without such a norm. A clue to the criterion of judgment lies in the various aspects of the demonic we have examined. These structures always mask and deform, and they ultimately destroy the person. They disrupt personal freedom and the power to grow toward greater freedom. I propose the following for a normative understanding of personal existence in freedom: The person is the free subject in whom the dimensions of love, power, and justice reinforce and enhance one another.

I make use here of one of Paul Tillich's great books, *Love, Power, and Justice,* in which he analyzes the relationships between these three structures, which are fundamental for all being, including human nature.[10]

A normative anthropology developed in this way makes it possible to discriminate between divine and demonic realities. Love is the spirit of universal outgoing and sharing of life with life. Power is the power of being, the dynamic energizing drive that is actualized in all becoming. Justice, the dimension so often overlooked, means the right ordering within the person of all the elements in body, mind, and soul so that there is a creative order in the person. It also means right order on the basis of loving concern between each subject and all other subjects, indeed with the whole of things.

The demonic powers try to pull love, power, and justice apart from each other. Power without justice and charity is oppression and violence.

Love without power or justice is sentimentality. As Rollo May wrote with great discernment: "Powerlessness corrupts."[11] Justice without love lacks the most important ingredient of justice itself, compassionate openness toward the other. A growing effective unity of these three dimensions of personal being is the test of victory over demonic corruption.

Such an analysis may help us to avoid a too simple moralism in the interpretation of personal and social history. The forms of creative life are often strange and dark. In the lives of creative artists a mysterious linkage often appears between the demonic realm and creative insight. Indeed, in the New Testament, the demons are credited with special knowledge. They recognize the Christ before humans do. The self-destructive side of the creative process seems to gain a foothold in some at least whose creativity is unquestioned. Franz Kafka depicted the demonry of inertial bureaucratic systems so powerfully that he helped a whole generation to see the truth although his own life was ridden with neurotic blockage and illness. A reviewer of his published letters remarks, "Apparently some transcendent artists have to pass through the needle's eye of neurosis to reach their particular destinies."[12] Agreed.

We cannot prescribe a single path, and certainly not a path without danger, to personal freedom for individuals and for societies. But the point is to pass through the needle's eye and not to fall into denying that at its center life has the urge toward wholeness, or into a demonic worship of established powers.

For this also characterizes the demonic structures: they always somewhere meet opposition. They are challenged precisely in their demonic character. A divine reality arises against them, is attacked by them, and counter-attacks. History is the scene of that clash.

2

Breaking the Demonic Power

The demons have power; that is why they are feared. They can only be
defeated by power; that is why they must be exorcised. Here we consider
how resistance against the demonic comes into human experience and
how the demonic power is broken.

We are dealing with a theme as full of mystery as the demonic itself.
The power to resist the demonic is not simply a human power but one
that grasps us from beyond ourselves, so that the experience of being
set free from bondage is an experience of a power greater than ourselves.
People have always made attempts to control the power of the divine
by various techniques. At their most naive level, these techniques are
magic and superstition. In the more developed levels of culture people
claim control over the sacred, an assumption that is itself demonic.

Therefore, when we speak of combatting the demonic, of exorcism,
and of victory over the demonic powers, we are not looking for techniques of control but for modes of openness to the power that can set
us free. Resources for the conflict can be identified, marshaled, and
trusted, but they do not consist of effective techniques. As orientations
of the spirit, they involve personal acts of internal confession and prayer
and public acts of individual and collective defiance.

We have said that the demonic plays upon fear, represses humanity
and courage, masks reality with untruth. But there are moments in
individual experience and in social history when demonic madness is
exposed and a new possibility of sanity is realized. Persons and societies
become whole.

We see such a moment in the healing ministry of Jesus, which clearly
included acts of exorcism. Persons who are possessed by demons—and

15

this could mean any kind of madness or illness we would recognize as destroying personal freedom and the unity of personality—encounter in the healer a power greater than the demons. The demons are driven out. Jesus seems to recognize more than one type of possession: "This kind never comes out except by prayer and fasting" (Matt. 17:21), he says in one instance when the disciples are frustrated. In his name his followers become exorcists and healers and report success: "Lord, even the demons are subject to us in your name" (Luke 10:17). Christian communities have always practiced exorcism, and the experience, often in extreme forms, continues today. Sects and groups both within and outside established religion practice it in special ways. Their explanations often seem to border on the magical, but the experience is real enough.

Public Resistance

My concern, however, is with the public aspects of the breaking of the demonic power in common life. It takes place in many forms and without the trappings of bizarre rituals. What the depth psychologists describe as crises of insight or clarification sometimes take dramatic form as occasions of being set free from possession. Some of us have experiences of combat with obsessive fears and neurotic habits that we have to face and overcome; in *The Fifty-Minute Hour,* psychiatrist Robert Linder describes the struggles of several people engaged in such conflicts.[1] These are analogous to the experience of liberation from the demonic.

In the realm of the social demonries we can find more public evidence of the divine overcoming the demonic. Experiences of public clarification and insight are accompanied by deliverance from the destructive power of the spells that hold cultures in their grips. One example is the seventeenth-century American witchcraft mania, broken by the restoration of sanity in Salem. Another is the Army-McCarthy hearings of the 1950s. Although Senator Joseph McCarthy held most of the nation in the grip of fear, some stood against him from the beginning. Edward R. Murrow defied him on the public medium of television. And through that same medium, the courageous prosecution by Joseph Welch destroyed McCarthy's power. Sanity returned. Likewise, in every religious tradition the established hierarchy may become oppressive. The leaders, as Reinhold Niebuhr said, may distill power from sanctity and threaten prophetic thought and feeling. But religious reformers can defy the sacral demonries. And where there is a great sacred power present in a single person, such demonries can be turned in a new direction.

All of this happens in part through the slow processes of history. In interpreting history, we must allow for the working of the divine as a gradual, patient education of humanity toward more fully personal freedom and humaneness in modes of life.

This must not lead us to a simple philosophy of progress in the overcoming of the demonic. Hitler's Germany arose in the midst of one of the most cultured and technologically superior nations in the world. The wiretapping paranoia in our present government[2] arose among a group of presumably intelligent, dedicated, thoughtful people who, curiously, had so much power they did not even need to fear losing an election. We shake our heads at the sheer stupidity of which we and others are capable. It is sometimes hard to draw a line between demonic behavior and plain fatuousness. But the demonic always has an element of paranoia in it. Ghosts are seen, skeletons rattle. Fear drives us to strange acts and to self-destruction.

Yet there is evidence that the divine power is also at work. The demonic aspects of commercialized sports exercise an enormous psychological and economic power, but we are beginning to get individual testimonies from some players. Perhaps some of them are disgruntled and therefore unfair in what they say; but the exposures suggest a free humanity arising against the system. Vince Lombardi was reported to have denied saying that winning is the only thing; instead, he claimed to have said, "The effort to win is the only thing." It is an improvement. The demonic hold of the sense of racial superiority over minds and cultures can be broken, sometimes by individuals, sometimes by a move to sanity in a culture so that the truth begins to be known and justice grows.

Identifying Tactics

In such instances, we are dealing with social and historical processes that have no final explanation except that there is a power making for sanity and freedom. It is the divine thrust toward wholeness at work. God works out the divine way in history, within our understanding but far beyond it, and God's clash with the demonic has depths we cannot fathom. We can be grateful for it, and we can try to see where it is and to provide conditions for its fuller working.

Acknowledging our limitations, we can identify certain common elements in the experience of facing and overcoming the demonic, elements that give guidance for a faithful resistance to what destroys our humanity. A power greater than the demons can be invoked. We

cannot control it, but we can know it and be reinforced by that knowledge. We shall speak of the courage of faith, of rituals of reinforcement,
and of the role of a love-informed reason.

The Courage of Faith

The most impressive single thread in the meeting of divine and demonic
power appears to be personal defiance of the demonic power through
a courage that fear cannot break and a truthfulness that lies cannot
destroy. Satan attacks the personal center. He wants to possess souls;
until the soul is possessed, the mind clouded, the heart made fearful,
the demonic cannot win. Hence the many classical images of Satan
bargaining for the soul. The biblical paradigm is the meeting of Christ
and Satan. The presence of this story in the Scripture is the supreme
expression of faith that the showdown between the divine and the
demonic comes at the center of personal being. The Christ who represents our humanity for the sake of redemption must meet—face-to-
face in mortal combat—the father of lies, the tempter, the destroyer.

It is the person, created in the image of God, capable of reason, love,
and hope, who is the carrier of the creative good in history. The power
of grace must work in that personal center to save human beings from
subservience to the demonic power. Tillich says, "Demonry breaks down
only before divinity, the possessed state before the state of grace."[3]

Often the demonic power is seen through and shattered by courageous
solitary individuals or very small groups. In the biblical tradition stand
the great prophets: lonely individuals, often imprisoned, derided, sometimes killed, who stand almost alone against a Baal-worshiping nation
or a national demonic ecstasy reinforced by idolatry. James A. Sanders
has suggested that the prophetic writings were preserved, and became
scripture, because in the time of the exposure of false hopes, in the time
of disillusionment, when the demonic ecstasy had been broken, people
remembered what the prophets had said.[4] Thus, the tradition of protest
and prophetic judgment becomes vital in the religious and political
establishment for the sake of the establishment's sanity.

At the center of the resistance to the demonic appears an absolute
courage, the personal courage of the individual or group standing against
the prevailing power, defying it at whatever cost, becoming the channel
of new insight in history. This is courage, not in the sense of a particular
and isolated virtue but in the sense in which Paul Tillich equated courage
with faith.[5] He sees "the courage to be" as the faith that "accepts our
being accepted" and thus allows freedom for life in the truth.

The divine re-creates the person in the face of the demonic. Many biblical injunctions witness to this, for they are designed to dispel fear. "Do not fear those who kill the body but cannot kill the soul; rather fear him who can destroy both soul and body in hell" (Matt. 10:28). That is, fear the divine, but the divine only. "Perfect love casts out fear" (1 John 4:18). "He who dwells in the shelter of the Most High [shall abide] in the shadow of the Almighty" (Ps. 91:1). "We will not fear though the earth should change, though the mountains shake in the heart of the sea" (Ps. 46:2).

Crucially important in this power of freedom from fear, this courage of faith that works toward overcoming the demonic, is the existential belief that there *is* power superior to the earthly powers. Martin Luther's hymn recognizes this:

> Did we in our own strength confide
> Our striving would be losing.

Yet we should never claim that belief in God as defined in some specific religious concept is essential to the freedom to defy the demonic. There is a courageous human will that can stand against demonic power without any certain confidence of aid by a higher power. But here we meet an issue that goes to the root of what religious faith means. The demonic appears first in religious guise, and all religions have asserted ways to salvation from the demonic grip. What religious faith has offered is the conviction that there exists a power superior to the demonic, a truth that can be found beyond the untruths. Satan always meets his match. This conviction makes the question of the meaning of religious faith for human culture so critical. We all sense, wherever we stand on that question, that something of utmost importance for our humanity is at stake.

If there is plausibility in the claim that belief in divine power, superior to the demons, reinforces human capacity to defy the demons, what are we to say about humanisms that appeal to no such power? Some see "man on his own," as Ernst Bloch has expressed it.[6] Or, in Albert Camus's *The Plague,* Dr. Rieux says we must have saints without God.[7]

I defend the following claim: Those who do not believe in God or in any divine power superior to humanity either fall into despair, or they assert the reality of some mode of life and some truth that stands in its own right beyond the distortions of the demonic. The saints without God are not nihilists. They stand on a truth that undercuts all lies and on an authentic human existence that is opposed to inauthentic life. These later terms are, of course, Martin Heidegger's. If authentic existence is not possible at all, there is no point in distinguishing between the authentic and the inauthentic.

So, for Jean-Paul Sartre, the person is a useless passion; he or she longs for God though there is no God. What keeps Sartre from nihilism is his recognition that there is a difference between good faith and bad faith. Unless that distinction can be made, there is no point to the Sartrean analysis of life and no meaning in the courage that he so often displayed in opposing human injustice, participating in the French Resistance and exposing the suffering of Algeria.

Ernst Bloch, whose philosophy stands behind much of the new theology of hope, says he is an atheist. Man is "on his own," without God. In his great book *Das Prinzip Hoffnung,*[8] he declares salvation for humanity through human becoming. Yet when Bloch, one of the most profound of the humanist philosophers, describes this pilgrimage of humanity, he acknowledges that he is talking not just about what a human being is but about the depths of creative life in which humans participate. He envisages an end or fulfillment, the kingdom of human freedom as a mystical community to be attained. When Bloch discloses his vision, he sees even death as overcome. We live on into a future in a kind of transmigration of souls.

When we have followed Bloch to the end, we discover his belief in a final victory of humanity in a transfigured freedom whose depth lies far beyond our present imagining. He seems close to saying that humanity participates in a reality greater than itself that makes possible its fulfillment. One wonders how to draw a distinction between this and the biblical faith that we are being transformed by grace into the divine image, and that "eye has not seen nor ear heard" what God has prepared for those who love him. If we ask Bloch whether he really believes that present-day humans become the new humanity through their will and effort alone, the question remains unanswered, though when he demythologizes the state he declares that in the better society there always must be a church. Bloch understands this as a community whose vocation it is to hold before humanity our spiritual nature, to affirm the final claims of the spirit in its reach beyond any conceivable present order, no matter how just and good it might be.

In relation to the demonic, religious faith is ambiguous. The demonries love religion, its ritual, belief, power, and sanctity. It is easily pressed into the service of the idols of power, money, prestige, and control. But the demonries also most fear religion; for religious faith at its root is a hold on a power that can resist the demonic. That power does not pass away. Though it cannot be controlled, it can be known, experienced, and relied upon. The apostle Paul's "Who will deliver me from this body of death? Thanks be to God . . ." (Rom. 7:24-25), and Luther's "Here I stand; I can do no other"[9]—these recall us to the sources of ultimate sanity and sustain the hope of a free and tolerable creative human existence. Paul Ricoeur says, "However radical evil may be it is not as primordial as goodness."[10] This conviction surfaces and becomes powerful when the demonic powers are finally challenged in history.

Ritual

A second element in the resistance against the demonic emerges from this analysis: religious ritual, which reinforces the courage of faith. The demonries live upon fear; they play upon it and excite it, including its sources in morbidity. This is one reason for the public show of cruelty, either overt or covert, that characterizes demonic social powers. They threaten, they punish, they hold up examples of their power to crush. We have only to remember the large role fear has played in religious control. The threats of hell and eternal punishment become demonic and are a major resource of Satan in his capacity to make people afraid. He fascinates and dominates in part by his cruelty. The divine power must use the resources of human ritual and association to set us free from fear.

Ritual reenacts the victory of the divine over the demonic, whether legendary or not; the words of Galileo spoken from the torturers' rack become a powerful cultural treasure. Punished for teaching that the earth revolves around the sun, that it is not at rest but moves, Galileo kept maintaining, "And still it moves." One fact, articulated by a sane mind and courageous spirit, can be fatal to the powers that be. But the power of that truth is enormously enhanced by its being remembered and celebrated in social groups.

Inner personal courage has its public rituals of celebration, acknowledgment, and reinforcement. The symbols of faith have to be internalized or else they are futile; but we have them as potent cultural heritage. There is no more private record of the soul in modern times than Dag Hammarskjöld's *Murkings*.[11] Few books go as deep into the abysses of the personal spirit. But the language Hammarskjöld finds for self-probing is the language of the Bible, the mystics, the church, and the tradition. Here the public ritual reinforces a private and internalized form, and the significance of public ritual in resistance to the demonic becomes visible.

One function of public worship is the practice of bringing into the open the demonic powers—naming them, identifying them, confessing their presence in us and around us, and drawing upon the central moments in our collective memory in which the demons have been exposed. But this function has faded into the background. The late Rabbi Abraham Heschel wrote of worship in Judaism:

> Services are conducted with dignity and precision. The rendition of the liturgy is smooth. Everything is present: decorum, voice, ceremony. But one thing is missing: Life. One knows in advance what will ensue. There will be no surprise, no adventure of the soul; there will be no sudden outburst of devotion. Nothing is going to happen to the soul. Nothing unpredictable must happen to the person who prays. He will attain no insight into the words he reads; he will attain no new perspective for the life he lives. Our motto is monotony. The fire has gone out of our worship. It is cold, stiff, and dead. True, things are happening; of course, not within prayer, but within the administration of the temples. Do we not establish new edifices all over the country?
>
> Yes, the edifices are growing. Yet, worship is decaying.[12]

We would not have to change a word to describe much of Christian worship.

Religiousness that tries to exorcise the demonic by ignoring it or denying its existence is very common, one might even say popular. Positive thinking has its place. It is possible to be morbidly absorbed in the forms of evil and in our fears of them; that is not constructive. But against all attempts to destroy the demons by denying them, the fact is that fears repressed return in other forms. The passion to declare that things are really all right can be driven by hidden fears. With denial of the demons comes a loss of freedom to face realities, a drift into sentimentality, with a corresponding lack of sensitivity to others' fears, since they tend to cause us to uncover our own.

Further, the denial of the demonic leaves us helpless before actual demonic social structures. We have no categories for understanding the exploiting character of social systems. This is why ignoring the demonic is likely to appear most attractive to those who profit from the established order. Those who suffer from it either cover up their hurt by accepting the situation, or they rebel. The rebellion can be ambiguous and may lead to the "demonizing" of the establishment in unjust ways, but no establishment is without its demonic aspects.

A liturgy that is rooted in the biblical witness and other profound literature of the tradition has the possibility of unmasking ourselves and our embedded social evils, of celebrating their exposure in the past, and of remembering the appearance of the divine power that judges all earthly principalities and powers. Profound worship moves toward a recovery of sanity in the midst of lies and distortions, but it can be had only at the price of honesty and a demand for reality, no matter how disturbing. It never cries " 'Peace, peace' when there is no peace" (Jer. 6:14).

Reason

In this analysis of what breaks the power of the demonic, I have put first the emotional factors that engage the whole of our being. The power to break the demonic must marshal all human powers, and the central ones are emotion, passion, and communal reinforcement. They enter into the courage of faith.

We turn now to the use of reason in combatting the demonic. Here lies a critical issue for our culture and for religion. What is the function of reason in dispelling the fears that the demonic powers and structures hold over us? Courage alone is not enough. The hallucination produced by the demonic powers has to be exposed, and that means that truth has to be recognized.

Rational criticism and analysis accomplish at least three major ends in relation to the demonic.

First, they dispel superstition about demonic personalized entities invading the world. This is an achievement of modern scientific reason. One of its victories was the attack on the belief in witches. Among members of the medical profession today, deep in the professional con-sciousness, is a memory of the witchcraft mania and the search to find understandable causes, both of the symptoms attributed to witchcraft and of the mania itself. The "witchhunt" is a perennial part of the pathology of human societies in religion and in politics. Belief in demons as supernatural powers can itself be demonic.

If we recognize that we do not in fact live in a universe populated by supernatural spirits who invade our personalities, if we in fact have more valid ways of understanding phenomena such as seizures, neuroses, and violent behavior that we observe in persons and societies, the

achievement of our new understanding is largely the result of the progress of scientific objectivity. We need not claim to explain completely
the mysterious pathological phenomena in order to keep probing for
such understanding as we can get. Some human cruelties are, as we say,
unbelievable. We can close our minds to what goes on in concentration
camps, in prisons, in the ghettos of our own cities. There remains a
will to know the truth, to understand, that can only function when we
have been relieved of superstitious bondage. That requires a dedication
to rational inquiry.

This applies to the social demonries. They produce hallucinations and
their own mythology of explanation, usually fastening upon some group
that can be blamed for the troubles. These hallucinatory mythologies
have to be exposed. The structures of demonic social power are des-
perately afraid of criticism and satire. They cannot stand it.

We know now that our own governing officials lied to us about many
things in connection with the Vietnam War and about Cambodia. We
know it because the instruments of repression are not yet strong enough
in our society to prevent the truth from being uncovered in some cases.
Freedom of speech and press will not prevent the social demonries from
taking control; but they are a major resistance against them, and that
is why such freedoms are so precious.

Humor is a rational faculty and another major defense of sanity. All
establishments produce a stream of underground humor, which in some
measure destroys the pretense and pomposity of the demonic claims.
During a recent election in Greece, a story went around that a voter
had gone into the voting place and was handed a sealed ballot to drop
in the box. He opened it, saying he would like to know for what or
whom he was voting. The official remonstrated, "How dare you! Don't
you know this is supposed to be a secret ballot?"

The use of reason in interpreting the causes and conditions of social
demonries is one of the prime scientific tasks of our time. After the
deluge, we try to understand what has possessed a people or a nation.
Hannah Arendt's account of the Eichmann trial is a classic instance of
the use of an informed, humane, scientific, and philosophical reason to
probe demonic power and its structure. She can speak rationally of the
"banality of evil." We have said the demons are interesting; they have
their fascination. In a sane human life the truth is, finally, *more* interesting, however hard it is for us to see it that way.

Some social scientists object to the use of the category of the demonic
because it suggests a mystique and a depth that reason cannot grasp,

which thus leads us away from concrete social analysis. We must appreciate this objection. But we still need the category to designate one kind of social structure that differs from others. The difference can be, in part, rationally described.

The sane society must be, in some measure, the open society. It must allow the possibility of rational criticism being given and being heard. This last qualification is critical in this time of mass media. The power of control in communications is beyond anything imagined in previous times. It lies behind the realistic fears of Orwell's *Nineteen Eighty-Four*.[13] What kinds of defense do we have against such power? Surely, that defense requires some kind of deliberate planning for social self-criticism, and that planning requires reasonable judgment. We have a token illustration of the problem and an honest attempt at an answer in the laws requiring equal time for opposing views on the mass media, and in provisions by broadcasters for replies to their editorials. The point is that the recognition of the demonic powers is itself a major reason for giving the fullest range to science, to rational criticism, to dispelling the myths that bolster the power of control over the mind and soul, and to rational construction (so far as we can achieve it) of constitutions, orders of life, and educational processes that set reason free.

When all this is done, however, we have further questions about reason. A rational analysis of reason shows that it is a function of personal existence and social power, as well as a critical resource against such power. Reason as an ideal can itself become infected with demonic pretension. "Ideology" is a word designating a threat that looms in every claim for the rational guidance of life. The purely rational state of Plato's *Republic* has a sinister overtone. Devotion to reason alone may be dehumanizing. One thinks of Descartes: "I am determined to accept nothing but what I can clearly and distinctly perceive to be true." This is an impossible program, and one that Descartes did not really carry out. Or recall Hegel's remark at the beginning of his lecture on the philosophy of history: He will lead his hearers to the result of the meaning of world history, "a result which happens to be known to me because I have traversed the entire field." The enthronement of the Goddess of Reason in the French Revolution was the celebration of an ecstatic liberation, but it was hardly the creation of a rational state. The Terror followed, and in twelve years Napoleon was crowning himself emperor in Notre Dame Cathedral.

We can assess the significance of reason, then, only by recognizing that it is never an independent function. Reason lives in persons and societies. It never has a purely independent role. One might put against this the example of logic and mathematics, though even here we have to recognize a history of the sciences and the awareness that there is no final system of mathematics or logic. In any case, when we deal with any concrete reality, we are involved in the appraisal of the processes of knowing in relation to the organic, emotional, personal life of persons and societies. The integration of the personality, the Jungians tell us, requires an integration of the self and its reason with the archetypal images that direct and shape the psyche. In some of Freud's earlier expressions, his system seemed to aim at rational clarification as the secret of human freedom; but the way to it involved far more than rational analysis, as Freud quickly discovered. Later, Freud and the neo-Freudians saw that the fulfillment of personal existence requires a uniting of *logos* with *eros,* reason with passion. Theologians would put their final evaluation of reason in the form "reason exists in order to love," and many psychiatrists would agree.

The understanding of demonic structures leads us to the decisive importance of the uniting of scientific, rational, and humanistic elements in culture. As C. P. Snow warned us, we are threatened with a split consciousness between scientific, technological, and humanistic values. If religion's function in life is to direct us to the roots of sanity through the rediscovery of the wholeness of the person and of our relationship to the divine, then reason has a final stake in the healing of the rent between intellect and feeling.

Sometimes the problem is put as follows: Science produces techniques but not values, so we need humanistic definitions of ends. But this does not overcome the split. Science and technology create ends, they make new values possible, they establish powers that alter the situation of value. Consider the technical means of controlling procreation and the possibility of genetic control. Humanistic study does not draw upon an esoteric realm of pure values floating above the concrete world. It should be a reflection on our present experience as it embodies the kinds of goals we do have, the consequences of modes of life we now adopt, the effect of the scientific mentality on human purposes. It should offer explanation of new possibilities and a criticism of the means-ends relationship as embodied in our present experience. Humanistic studies employ reason to explore the depths of the rational and irrational in human experience.

Atomic weaponry is a supreme achievement of rational knowledge, the organization of theory and production for the construction of weapons, but it produces a need for rational, sane control to avoid accidents and wanton destruction. *The Bulletin of the Atomic Scientists* has, from the beginning of its publication, reflected the profound struggle of scientists to apply a rational morality to the possession of such weapons. The competition in weaponry has its demonic aspects. Each nation is driven to become stronger than the others, until each has an overkill potential astronomical in its proportions. But the search for rational methods of control must go on.

I believe that litanies in praise of reason and science have their place in the support of a human culture. The religious traditions, on the whole, have been much too slow in celebrating the achievements of reason against superstition. A line from Joseph Addison's hymn to the stars,

"In reason's ear they all rejoice"

has too few counterparts in the official liturgies. But we have already noted that the purging and fulfillment of reason involves the wholeness of personal existence. There must be a purgation of the passions, and an evocation of the courage to hear and speak the truth. Therefore, we must look to the passionate philosophers, artists, and poets who bring rational perception into the light and service of personal courage and love.

Friedrich Nietzsche had his demonic side, as do many great artists, but Nietzsche's exploration of shallow idealism, his breaking through the absurdities of a sentimentalized religious culture, his extraordinary perception of the appeal of religion to the weaker sides of human nature—all this is informed by the passion of protest articulated in the light of superbly perceptive intellect.

In our day, some of those who have given us resources of imagination against the demonic are writers and artists of great intellectual power, who use art to give form to the dark fears that cloud our lives and give entrée to the demonic. Franz Kafka draws a picture of demonic bureaucratic order in which everything is ordered in a superbly technical perfection, the result of which is insanity. It is drawn with great rational control. No contemporary artist depicts the grip of fear and the darkness of the irrational threat in existence more powerfully than Samuel Beckett. In the play *Endgame* and novels such as *Molloy*,[14] we are given compelling descriptions of what it means to see existence as absurdity, yet with a longing for love. No artist of our time creates with a more perfect sense of form, a more remorseless intellect, and a more passionate demand to see the truth.

If the demonic is to be overcome it must be met and known. I recall Herman Melville's remark about Claggart, the persecutor of Billy Budd: In order to move from a normal nature to a man like Claggart, you "have to cross the deadly space between." The crossing of that space requires a courageous exploration inspired by more than the rational desire to know, but it requires rational analysis and understanding, not its abandonment. Reason must seek an illumination of that which threatens humane existence, get it out into the open, and draw its outlines for us to recognize.

Surely, this is why the great artists often live on a borderline between sanity and the dark realm of the unknown and disordered. In the New Testament, the demons are credited with extraordinary insight. They recognize the Christ while his messiahship is still a secret among ordinary humanity. We are touching upon a theme that leads us to the danger zones of our psychic life. Some today argue that the real indicators of the dynamics in contemporary experience are found among the so-called pathological phenomena. R. D. Laing has made much of this in his thesis that it is the schizophrenics who disclose to us the dynamics of our experience. A rational analysis will show that Laing's thesis has a kernel of truth amid considerable exaggeration. He does point us to a critical matter with which this analysis of the breaking of the demonic presents us: There is no breaking the spell of the power of the demonries without the marshalling of the whole force of human courage in the will to face the demon with humane insight and with hope for overcoming.

The great dramatic artists and poets not only depict demonic possession, they live from a faith that demonic power can be broken. Most contemporary drama, even where it plunges toward madness at some point, calls us to see through the hallucination and to repossess our souls. Edward Albee in *Who's Afraid of Virginia Woolf?*[15] has "fun and games" for the theme of the first act, "Walpurgisnacht" for the second (in which a couple who has been surviving by creating an imaginary son reach a height of destructive fury), and for the last act, "the exorcism." Some illusions are dispelled by the end of the play; there is a kind of resolve for a new future. Hardly to be called redemption, it is a catharsis and clarification. The demons have been faced, some overcoming has been experienced, and the demons have not won.

Samuel Terrien, an extraordinarily sensitive interpreter of the modern arts, finds in contemporary painting the kind of penetration to the core of meaning that I am seeking to express:

> Modern artists discern within natural and historical evil the sign of
> the pathos of being. Paul Klee writes, "Art is a likeness of creation.

The heart that beats in this world seems mortally wounded to me."
Such a remark brings to mind the biblical vision of the spirit, dovelike,
hovering "over the vast abyss," and bringing, at a cost, life out of
chaos. Modern painting points not to the created things but to creation
itself. And that is the reason why it does not exclude what conventional
aesthetics called "the ugly." The beautiful is always exclusive of the
ugly. The modern painter, like the modern theologian, turns his gaze
toward the totality of being and denudes, unveils, unmasks man from
all his pretenses, and then seeks the depths of beauty which always
remain within the ugly.[16]

In contemporary dramatists who seem to parody the Eucharist in modes
that are overtly blasphemous, Terrien sees a probing to the deepest levels
of both our need and our hope. Interestingly, he uses the image of the
willingness to transgress the limits of sacred space. Perhaps that is necessary if we are to cross deadly spaces to our own deepest conflict with
the demons. Terrien writes:

> Elemental anxiety is the key to the drama of sacrilege. Profanation is
> the daring to transgress the limits of the sacred space—and nothing
> is to be lost thereby. Man faces the ultimate of being by risking his
> all. When the playwrights of the Absurd place blasphemy at the center
> of the stage, they are not simply rebelling against a corrupt society;
> they are returning to the ritual roots of drama. In their hands, the
> theatre of revolt becomes again the theatre of communion.[17]

The cultural resource to which we must turn for the exorcism we
crave is the literature of the world that moves across deadly spaces and
is not trapped by it. The Bible viewed thus is the supreme instance of
the religious experience, which surfaces the demonic forces, which names
Satan, and which declares for the greater power of grace. The great
literature of the world, from the Greek tragedians and Shakespeare to
the character of Willy Loman in Arthur Miller's *Death of a Salesman,*
does its final work in the renewal of our capacity to see through the
tragedy into some ultimate greatness. Sheer distillation of horror lacks
final authority.

In the view of our analysis, we would have to say this is because
horror alone never quite tells the truth: there would be no perception
of horror unless we had some insight into the glory. The boredom and
the horror and the glory, to use T. S. Eliot's words, are *all* present when
we see truly. Great literature reconstitutes our perceptions in the direction of sanity.

Herein lies our hope, that in the very experience of demonic possession we discover a superior power working against it—often silently, hidden, and at times apparently impotent, yet now and again breaking through to restore us to our rightful minds. This is true in psychological therapy, in political and economic struggle, in religious frenzy and faith, and at those final boundaries of life and death when "perfect love casts out fear" (1 John 4:18).

3

War in Heaven

One of the most important reflective books to come out of the Second World War is *The Warriors,* by an American philosopher, J. Glenn Gray, who was in American intelligence and went through the Italian campaign. His book on facing death and life, on love and violence, moves through the arena of life under supreme stress. In the conclusion he reflects upon the whole experience:

> War reveals dimensions of human nature both above and below the acceptable standards for humanity. In the end, any study of war must strive to deal with gods and devils in the form of man. It is recorded in the holy scriptures that there was once war in heaven, and the nether regions are still supposed to be the scene of incessant strife. Interpreted symbolically, this must mean that the final secrets of why men fight must be sought beyond the human, in the nature of being itself.[1]

"War in heaven" is recounted by the prophet Isaiah and in the Book of Revelation. We have begun our inquiry on the plane of concrete experience. We have sought the actuality of demonic power and its overcoming in the common life. We cannot experience this existential conflict without asking further questions. How do the demonic powers get into the world? What is their relationship to the divine power that we identify as creative? Do we adopt a dualistic view of reality, in which the divine contends with an intractable opposition? Do we follow the gnostic way to salvation and see the present world as fallen into the grasp of alien powers that are sometime to be overcome in a cosmic revolution?

31

In the biblical description, Satan is an angel in the heavenly host. He rebels against God, yearns for a higher status, battles the divine in heaven, and is cast out to take his revenge by tempting and thus threatening to destroy God's creatures, humankind. How are we to take such a tale? If it is a mythological expression of ultimate truth, what truth? Something may be disclosed here about how things really are. The mystery of the demonic is the mystery of a disruption of human life at the deepest levels of feeling and thought. Whatever salvation can be, it must be salvation from the hold of demonic power. The Christian Scriptures claim that God has already broken the powers, has won his victory over them. Yet life goes on. Death and sin and violent destruction are still our lot. Are we left with only a promise of final victory, the binding of Satan at the end? If so, can we give meaning to an end of history?

Many theologies cautiously stay with the traditional symbols, interpret them as best they can, and leave their mystery to be unveiled at the last day. "Now I know in part; then I shall understand fully, even as I have been fully understood" (1 Cor. 13:12). Perhaps it is a wise reticence. Yet I think we must take a further step and try to say what we hold to be the ontological meaning of the war in heaven and of its consequences. I do not think we can avoid the question of the ontological status of evil. My interest is not purely theoretical, as if we must guess at answers to questions we can't help asking, but arises out of existential necessity. We cannot have an authentic human existence unless we know what we take to be real.

"What is real?" involves the question of what the risks of life mean. I want to explore this issue of risk, for it underlies our question about the ontological status of the demonic.

"Our Shelter from the Stormy Blast"

All religious faith offers some kind of security. Without the assurance of a meaning for life that nothing can take away, we do not have what religious faith has always professed to give. Without the security of participation in a power that is not finally subject to obstruction, we cannot see life as anything but absurd. There is too much tragedy, too much apparently meaningless suffering, too much agony amidst dark evil for us to see life as worthwhile unless there is some real good that counts, now and forever. At the end of his Uppsala lecture, "Create Dangerously," Albert Camus says, "Every great work (of art) makes the human face more admirable and richer, and this is its whole secret," and in his concluding sentence he says, "Each and every man builds for all."[2] This character of the human condition (to seek a lasting good) cannot be taken away. It is the truth of our being. It is that element of justification touched with hope that sustains the human venture.

Camus's lecture, however, speaks about something besides hope and security, something without which we do not really acknowledge our authentic being: risk. There is no real humanity without risk, and there is no creativity without danger. Here we have the two sides of the deepest issue for every religious faith: Is being itself, our being and that of all things, involved in risk? If so, what is risked and how?

Most traditional theology, both Eastern and Western, has affirmed an ultimate security in which the victory of the divine over the demonic is complete and certain and, in a sense, known in advance. It has offered peace in the finality of a total transcendence of strife. Sometimes this is described as participation in a reality above all time and separateness: The soul discovers its identity with Brahma in Hinduism; it achieves the state of nondifferentiation, nonseparating, in the Buddhist Nirvana; it dwells in the heaven of pure contemplation of God as described in Dante's *Paradiso*. Either above history or at the end of history is the final Sabbath rest that leads to no new first-day creation.

So attractive to life and faith is this vision that to challenge it seems blasphemous. For some, however, the possibility of faith depends on a revision of this tradition. This view of God's absolute and final disposal of all opposition implies the doctrine that from the beginning, God has intended the whole history of good and evil as it is. For if the absolute victory at the end is implied by omnipotence, then the whole must have been willed by that same omnipotence. The omnipotent and omniscient God must know what is to happen before it happens, and must permit whatever happens. So the war in heaven is really an incident in the divine plan. Satan's rebellion is within the divine providence. Its outcome is known; Satan's defeat is guaranteed from the beginning.

We ask why, if the end is known and the victory sure, there must be the ages of struggle and suffering. The answer is given by St. Augustine, and echoed by most traditional theologies in one way or another: The world is more beautiful because of the war in heaven and its consequences, more glorious because there has been the darkness of alienation and its overcoming by the perfection of love. St. Augustine uses all his dialectical skill to show how opposites enhance one another, how we can perceive the beautiful only against the ugly, the precious against the worthless.[3] We are almost persuaded by the argument, for we recognize in experience that the deepest good is tinged with the shadow of its opposite. Augustine wants to show that this truth holds even when the shadow includes the damnation to eternal hell of Satan and of all sinners who fall outside grace and do not repent. Thus, Dante sees inscribed over the gate of hell: "Divine love created this. Abandon hope all ye who enter here."

Augustine has one further metaphysical idea in his doctrine, favored by all Platonisms: that evil is nothing positive in itself. It is the nonbeing toward which created things or persons plunge when they turn away from God, who is being itself. In a sense, no real power opposes God; there is only the loss that attends departing from God, and that loss is simply loss of being. This view has played a fairly large role in classical religion and in many modern sects that affirm that what is good and perfect is real, and that evil is only ignorance or misunderstanding. But this view is unstable. One still has to ask how ignorance and illusion arise. They must have some actuality or some power, otherwise they are not worth attacking.

Universalist theologies move beyond some of the tension in this view by affirming that the salvation of all creation and of all persons is implied by the divine grace and power. In our time, Karl Barth has overcome some of the grimmer aspects of Calvin's doctrine of double predestination here by coming close to a universalist affirmation without quite accepting it.

Hallowed by time and acceptance as these doctrines are, they never resolve their deepest difficulty. The trouble with these assurances is that they purchase peace at the cost of eliminating all risk from humanity and from God. If genuine freedom involves risk and loss, then traditional theology leaves us unfree. If genuine creativity involves the uncertainty of not knowing the outcome beforehand, not having it guaranteed, then traditional theology takes away from God the creator's greatest dignity and glory, which is not absolute power to make everything come out right, but absolute love that involves God in the risks of an unfinished and suffering world.

In a world where there are genuine possibilities of good and evil, an internal reformation of faith itself is required. This idea has not yet been articulated in the religious traditions. I shall try to take a step toward a new position: *There is a risk in the divine creativity, a risk for God and a risk for God's creatures*. The appearance of demonic distortions and perversions is part of that risk. We have to ask what the ontological status is of the demonic structures and powers that appear within the divine creativity. And we have to look in a new way at the question of final hope for the victory of the divine over the demonic.

This revision of traditional theology may be approached in two fundamental ways. One is metaphysical, through the concept of being. The other is existential, through personal forms of experience. The metaphysical way requires assessment of the relation of possibility and actuality in God. The existential way involves interpretation of the meaning of love as creative freedom. In the end, these two arguments involve each other.

Risk in Divine Being

If actual being is a process, if time is real, if *to be* is *to become* in interaction with other beings, then actuality involves possibility. This concept is so much a part of our ordinary experience that it is astonishing how lightly most theologies and metaphysical systems have dealt with possibility. The reason is clear: They have regarded the merely possible as ontologically less worthy or significant than actual being. The possible belongs to transience, to time, to what may or may not be. For all Platonisms, the possible is an inferior order of being.

Yet, what would our human life be if there were no decisions involving alternate possibility, no movement into what is not yet fully actualized, no surprise or enjoyment of the newly discovered, no threat of the unknown, and no hope for the yet to be realized? This is not to make unpredictability in itself a higher value. It is to recognize the experienced possibility of new qualities of enrichment, and to appreciate that which gives zest, depth, tragedy, and hope to life.

Caring for another person would not have the quality it does if we knew that nothing new could befall the other or the relationship. It is the risk of loss that calls forth courage. All greatness, Camus says, is rooted in risk. If that is true about human life, then we have to ask whether religion serves either humanity or divinity by denying that God takes any risk in the creation of free and finite beings. In biblical theology, finitude is not evil. All have seen that. But we have to say what the positive values of finitude are that accompany the risk of creativity. Finitude means having to choose between incompatibles, having to accept loss for the sake of gain. This is the structure of life and of good. Surely even God must respond to concrete situations within the limits inherent in a finite world.

It may appear that we return to a dualism between good and evil possibilities, only now we have located the dualism in God's very self. Are we any further advanced in our thinking if we make God responsible for the demonic powers? This is the critical metaphysical issue for religion that accepts risk, and I believe it can be met. Evil possibilities are real, but they do not have the same ontological status as the good, for three fundamental reasons.

The first was recognized by St. Augustine long ago, and here I stand with him. Nothing can *be* without goodness, the pattern of perfection, the vital power of being; for to be is to be a value, a unification of structures, in order to embody a positive good. There is no being apart from the integration of structures, that is, truth; and the exemplification of something enjoyable and appreciable, that is, beauty.

Therefore, the possibilities of evil, which are real enough, are possibilities in the distortion of some positive good. To speak mythologically, Satan is a parasite. He has no independent standing of his own, no power of being. The demonic feeds on the divine power of being and distorts it. This does not mean the demonic is nothing, or that it does not acquire power over the good structures in some measure. It means that, of itself, the demonic has no independent power; the good does have such being in itself.

The second reason for the different ontological status of the demonic follows from the first. The demonic always moves toward final self-destruction. It cannot destroy the creative good, though it can destroy particular structures of good.

This becomes a critical point in the question of hope for final victory. There is a truth in the traditional formulations. The divine power outlasts every power that in any way blocks it. God moves behind and within every moment of existence with a patient, untiring, undefeatable thrust toward the clarification of judgment, the exploration of new good, and the fulfillment of creatures. The demonic structures have power, but not the same kind of staying power. This may seem a difficult affirmation to justify. Yet it is not incompatible with reflection on human history. It does not mean that the demonic gradually disappears from history, but that the demonries do get exposed and that a creative power of sanity reasserts itself.

A third differentiation between the demonic and the divine is this: Creative life can exploit demonic power, even the destructive power of evil, for the creation of new good.

The theodicies have always tried to show that the last word about any evil, tragedy, or loss cannot be spoken until the whole history is told. In our personal histories we make new beginnings and discover new depths through agonizing losses. In the arts, the human scene in its tragedy is often used to help us see more deeply into ourselves and into the great good always about to be born yet eluding us. Antigone, Hamlet, and Prince Mishkin (in Dostoyevsky's *The Idiot*) do not offer mere resolutions of human problems. They offer much more, giving insight into the truths that only emerge through tragic experience. We have to go beyond Aristotle's doctrine of catharsis to a theory of transfiguration. We experience the good in fragments. We can, by the grace of illumination, see those fragments as reflection of the absolute good that is always beyond the present.

Is an authentic faith possible that knows both the assurance of forgiveness and a hope beyond death, that accepts the risk of creativity arising in the divine life from which we come? Can such a faith release the will to create dangerously and yet sustain a final trust in life? We can only find out by risking ourselves and trying this way.

This means that the true valuation of any action can never be completed until its effects are known. In our human experience, actions can be judged as evil here and now, but the possible consequences of any action for new good always lie partly beyond us. Therefore, the final judgment and evaluation of the world's actions lie in God, who is the ultimate recipient of the effects of the world's action and who responds out of an unlimited, impartial, and suffering receptivity. In the old theology God wills Satan's actions. In this new theology God does not will them, and God is not at their mercy. They are known to the divine wisdom in their character as destructive; and that very knowledge, communicated in human experience, becomes a source of creative power.

This exploration of possibility and actuality so far is in the mode of metaphysical reflection on what it means to be, to become, and to experience good and evil in the temporal passage. It is not necessary to attribute any action in the world exclusively to God. Not all turns out for the greater good. The decisions of life reflect the dignity and freedom of human existence, and they are real decisions with consequences. Yet in every decision, we act within a reality that has an ultimate character that shines through every particular good, a character that includes a final assurance of participation in what is real in all being, all desires, and all hope.

Creative Freedom as Love

There is another approach to the redefinition of the relation between God and the demonic. It is derived from the biblical assertion that God's goodness is God's love. The meaning of love in human experience and in the being of God is not an abstraction of the "good" but is the real good: It is to be found in that mode of being, known in innumerable contexts, that has a final unity, the name of which is love. Among many ontologies of love, St. Augustine's is the most notable in our tradition. But once we have found an alternative to St. Augustine's identification of God with being-itself, the relationship of love to the demonic possibilities can be explored in a new way.

The heart of the matter is the relationship of love to the risks of freedom and to the modes of creativity. Love is impossible without freedom. Love is self-giving, out of concern for the other and for the relationship with the other. Love compelled is not really love. Depth psychology has given us abundant evidence that compulsiveness, the will to dominate, and the refusal of freedom to the other often wear the masks of love but are not love. Love requires the freedom of the self to be, to enjoy, to appreciate, and to create. It is the will and capacity also to set the other free to become. Love that does not will the free response of the other is counterfeit. This seems a commonplace concept today, though we have a difficult time living by it. But its theological consequences and implications for religious faith have yet to be explored.

A further aspect of this understanding of love is that freedom involves risk. Given the freedom of the self to grow and become, no one can predict absolutely what we will become. The authentic self must accept this. In loving, one is asking the other to accept risk. And the other moves also into an unknown future. There are open spaces in every loving relationship, possibility as well as actuality. Moreover, not only do those who love enter an unknown future, they enter the world that is love's context and has its own history. We love in the midst of titanic forces of nature, society, and history that shape life and destiny far beyond our planning or control.

We can take one further step and see that the creativity of love arises in freedom and risk. The story of life is one of coping with the moving processes of the world; of love accepting, risking, and creating its world of meaning in the midst of these processes in the history of love in the world.

Creativity is a profound mystery. We cannot simply equate creativity with love, for we have accepted that there is a demonic creativity. The conditions of human creativity are still largely unknown. What we can say is that creativity without love is self-destructive; a loving openness to the world, to persons, and to the risk of the future constitutes the authentic creative context. An actor says, "To play a role is to have a love affair with an audience." A musician says, "I love music. It keeps me alive." We live by our loves, fragmentary and broken as they are, whereas, as St. Augustine says, "the demons have knowledge without charity."[4]

If creativity that is not self-destructive requires the risk of love, does this not lead us to reflection on the divine creativity?

God must be open to an adventure with the world. There is a mystical tradition that holds that the act of creation was an act of withdrawal that left the finite world without the fullness of divine actualization. Old Testament interpreter Samuel Terrien has suggested that a divine pathos is manifest as a somewhat muffled but real countertheme in the biblical story of creation. The creation story can be read not as a pure act of omnipotence but as an act of creative love bringing into being that which will not be absolutely controlled. God says, "You must not eat of this tree that yields knowledge of good and evil. On the day you eat from that tree you shall die" (au. trans. of Gen. 2:17). But Adam and Eve do eat, and they do not die. To create a spiritual being in the divine image of God is a risk for the creatures and for God. It is this inescapable character of risk in love that drives us to reexamine the theological tradition.

Here metaphysical analysis and the phenomenology of love come together. Dynamic actuality is unthinkable apart from possibility. Possibility implies freedom, so that loving being is unthinkable apart from assuming the risk of decisions, self-giving, and creative life in an unfinished history.

I accept an ontology of love in the sense that being involves the mutual reinforcement of diverse entities. Love is the ultimate personal expression of that pattern. Being and love are not identical; but creative being is the expression of the spirit of love, taking the risks involved.

In referring to the biblical doctrine of creation, I have opened up the question of the relationship of a doctrine of divine risk in creation to biblical faith. Some are deeply engaged in that inquiry now, and to state a conclusion without entering upon the entire discussion is itself a risk. My view is that the theme of divine risk is not only present in the Scripture but is one of its dominant motifs. There is another strand in the Scripture that reflects the notion of the divine monarch with absolute omnipotence. Alfred North Whitehead argued that this was an inheritance from oriental despotism; the church gave God the attributes of Caesar. I do not think Whitehead is entirely wrong about this, but he failed to recognize another conception running throughout the Scriptures, that of the God who persuades the world, and in risk, draws it back in freedom to God's self. It is often obscured by the image of the absolute monarch, but again and again the view breaks through that

God makes God's self vulnerable to what humanity does, suffers from it, and brings new good out of the risk of freedom to create or in creating a new community of love and justice.

Risk-Taking Faith

Clearly we are dealing with unresolved questions and are moving in an area where we see as in a glass darkly. We are exploring the possibility of conceiving the life of faith as an acceptance of real conflict between the divine and the demonic powers. In this understanding faith becomes participation in the history where that struggle goes on, a participation that involves free response without knowing the outcome. It is trust in the divine without asserting that God has planned it this way or that the demonic is the divine in disguise. Paul Tillich says that in the divine being the divine and the demonic are one. I am denying that doctrine, and thereby making a break with most of the theological tradition. I affirm the possibility of a religious commitment and faith that acknowledges the reality of demonic perversion of the power of being and yet remains trusting and at peace in the face of unknown possibilities.

In the motion picture *Sounder,* the story of a family of black sharecroppers during the Depression of the 1930s, the husband, driven by his family's hunger, steals. He is caught and sentenced to a prison camp for a year. The greatest injustice is that the authorities refuse to tell his family where he is imprisoned, so they can have no communication with him. The family is visited by a minister in the community; with utmost sincerity and goodwill, he brings the conventional religious assurance that God must have a purpose in this, and that the family should trust that God's will is being done. The role of the mother is played by Cicely Tyson, and I believe she should have received the Academy Award, if for nothing else than her facial expression when she hears these conventional words of assurance. It is respectful, open, yet utterly rebellious. This word she will *not* take; she will not believe that God's justice is being done. Her expression in that moment is what my discussion here is all about. I am defending a view of religious and biblical faith in which one does not have to find comfort in the assurance that everything that happens is according to the will of God.

The question of assurance is acute. We have already said that one major source of strength in opposing the demonic is the belief that there is superior power in the divine. Whitehead says religion in its depth is not "a research after comfort."[5] Nevertheless, religion does lead to peace, as Whitehead also affirms. We need to examine how this kind of faith would stand in the presence of demonic power as it bears upon guilt, death, and a final victory. On the first of these questions (guilt), we may take a positive position; on the second (death), a more agnostic position; and on the third (final victory), a definite rejection of the tradition in favor of a new doctrine of endless creativity and risk in God. At this point it is possible only to indicate the issues involved in these three questions, not to develop them further.

We can be assured that mercy overcomes guilt. All the great religious traditions offer some kind of forgiveness and mercy that covers or transcends humankind's evil and alienation. Even the Karmic doctrine has the hope of salvation at the end, for nothing finally stands in the way of the person's attainment of ultimate union. Mahayana Buddhism, particularly the Amida tradition, has given Kwannon (Kwan-Yin), the goddess of mercy, a special place in the divine order.

In biblical faith our alienated humanity is thoroughly dependent on grace. One can put the logic of the assurance of faith quite simply: We are always assured of that which overcomes guilt, because we have already known it. Unless we say that there is never any mercy in experience, we cannot deny its possibility at any time or in any circumstance.

That the divine does have mercy is, in the religious traditions, affirmed on the basis not of sheer hope but of past and present experience. Love without mercy is unthinkable, and if to be is to participate in love, there is no being without mercy.

This assurance, and the concrete overcoming of guilt to which it leads in experience, is still a mystery, with all the complex processes involved in interpersonal relationships and in religious experience. We could explore the thesis that demonic powers live, in part, from the energies stemming from guilt. They exploit guilt and use it for many kinds of self-destructive psychological and social patterns. There are also demonic, perverted forms of forgiveness. When liturgies of repentance become substitutes for real repentance, grace becomes cheap grace, as Dietrich Bonhoeffer recognized. But mercy remains one of the present sure signs of divine reality and lasting hope.

Forgiveness does not set aside judgment, it requires it. It is the assurance there is a divine judgment that rests upon all life, a judgment that never rejects the possibility of a creative move beyond the past and present actuality. The fear of rejection drives us to our destruction; we build defenses against being caught, against being known, against risking ourselves to love, because we are afraid of consequences, afraid of one another, afraid of God's judgment. Forgiveness is not a passive covering over of wrong; it is the declaration of a new possibility. Accepting forgiveness requires a new risk and a new courage, as Paul Tillich makes clear. Assurance and courage belong together.

The reality of death presents a more complex issue. This is in part because we do not know what lies beyond death, and in part because death wears so many guises. It is difficult to know what we are really talking about, beyond an obvious biological fact, when we speak of the meaning of death or of hope in the face of death. There is, of course, a tradition that death exists in the world because of the Fall. It is a consequence of the demonic temptation and it symbolizes demonic power. It can be named the Last Enemy, as the apostle Paul calls it. But for Christian faith, the word death designates something more than the close of earthly life. It has become a sign of alienation, and even of a cosmic bondage.

Again, there is in the life of faith a victory over both the fear of death and the alienation that death has come to symbolize. Milton declares in *Paradise Lost*: "Suffering for Truth's sake is fortitude to highest victorie, and to the faithful, Death the Gate of Life."[6] This conviction is reaffirmed countless times in human experience, as in the words Bonhoeffer is reported to have said just before his execution: "This is the end, for me the beginning of life." This confident trust surely does not seem to depend on any one conception of what lies beyond death. It seems rather a trustful acceptance of the reality of death and a yielding up of life to the sustaining divine processes however they are conceived. The demonic powers are defeated at the moment when death is accepted, because death then destroys neither courage nor hope.

We must consider the question of a final event in which satanic power is destroyed forever, and eternal blessedness and peace fill the city of God. The tradition also declares that there will be a last state at the end of the divine history. This declaration undoubtedly fulfills something of our craving for clean beginnings and endings, especially in a history so filled with misery and wreckage. Wolfhart Pannenberg has argued that biblical faith requires the assurance that there be a final realization in which the essence of all things, which is God's being itself, becomes identical with what has come to be; without this realization, he says, the question of history is unresolved and faith loses the assurance of the divine victory that rightly belongs to it.

The metaphysical and religious doctrine I have been expounding collides decisively with Pannenberg's view. If divine love risked untold eons of creativity in this cosmic epoch to bring forth life and sensitivity and human comradeship, there is no reason to believe that the creative

spirit should not or will not continue to move from actuality to possibility, exploring the wonder of creation in new histories of freedom,
growth, conflict, and resolution.

Must there always be war in heaven? We do not know. But if this
potentiality rests on a true perception of faith—that the creative ground
of all things, God, will always risk the *possibility* of war in heaven for
the sake of new history of actualized love—then such a view is not only
compatible with the life of faith as trust in the lasting worth of life; it
may also be more interesting than the traditional view that the end is
assured from the beginning. That it is interesting may not be an argument for its truth, but it is surely not an argument against it.

PART TWO

Hope's Challenge
to Evil

4

Mystery and Hope

In the Christian faith the element of mystery that accompanies our hope is explicitly affirmed. We look into a future that lies beyond our knowledge. Paul says, "Who hopes for what he sees?" (Rom. 8:24). Yet the mystery is not sheer darkness. We anticipate what is to come on the basis of our present faith and knowledge. The mystery of God's will has been disclosed, though not completely. The perplexing assertions that the Bible makes about Christ's coming again, the Last Judgment, resurrection, and eternal life have meaning because they arise out of what God has already made known to us. At the same time, through the very character of God's self-disclosure in Jesus Christ we become even more deeply aware of the limitations of our knowledge. Thus, the questions about "last things" are not only questions about a future beyond our sight. They are questions about the depth of meaning of what God says to us in Jesus Christ. That is why Paul declares that hope abides, along with faith and love (1 Cor. 13:13).

The question of how we know God must continually be answered as we give our Christian witness, and it must be answered with fidelity both to God's word in Jesus Christ and to the facts of human experience. The question of *how we know* takes on special difficulties when we speak of Christian hope, for here we are most obviously reaching beyond our present experience. The difficulties involved become evident in the second statement on Christian hope of the advisory commission preparatory to the Evanston Assembly of the World Council of Churches.[1] The report asserts the authority of the Bible as the book that "speaks a sovereign language which compels attention and obedience and transforms and renews the mind." Yet when it comes to the eschatological

47

questions, the report cautions us against "a literal acceptance of the whole biblical imagery and symbolism." The biblical words, we are told, must be "translated" if the Christian hope is to be intelligible today.

Why is this so? It is not only because language changes. It is because we have to reckon with crucial shifts in our present understanding of time, nature, and the future course of the physical creation. We know through our experience that the "end of the world" of which many biblical writers speak was not imminent, as they expected. To be sure, we in our turn cannot be too dogmatic about the course of physical nature; but whatever predictions our scientific knowledge permits certainly involve a long-term process with laws of the dissipation of energy operating, and perhaps with processes of the renewal of energy systems operating as well. If a cosmic accident or atomic explosion were to destroy this earth, the destruction would have to be interpreted by a modern mind as involving physical causes (though of course we would not be around to do the interpreting).

In our discussion of Christian hope, we have to try to keep clear the distinction between what we know and what we don't know, and this is a difficult thing to do. Our declaration of Christian hope should be based on what we know and not on our ignorance. Therefore, before discussing the content of Christian hope, I shall try to explain what I take to be the basis of Christian knowledge.

Human Experience and
Christian Faith

The clue to Christian truth is that God's self-disclosure in Jesus Christ must come together with a critical understanding of our human experience in an intelligible unity of meaning. God makes God's self known through creation; but our decisive understanding even of God as Creator comes only through the special word that God has communicated by entering our human history in a personal life. We believe this happened in the life, death, and experienced resurrection of Jesus of Nazareth. God's self-disclosure in Jesus Christ is a penetration of our humanity, not a destruction of it. The truth God has given in Christ is that in which all truth coheres, as the New Testament says. Therefore what God's word in Christ means is truth, which we can have only through a continual reappropriation of it in the light of a critical reflection upon all our experience.[2]

If we discover that certain literal statements in the Bible cannot be brought into congruence with our understanding of nature as we experience it, then we shall have to reserve judgment and rethink the meaning of our Christian declarations until some more inclusive meaning emerges. This is not a question of importing an "alien" natural theology into our faith as a norm above the biblical truth. It is simply our acknowledgment that the truth of God's redemptive love in Jesus Christ is a saving truth for us precisely because it illuminates and fulfills all honest searching after the realities of our existence.

If we determine to be faithful to all the evidence when we express our Christian hope, one consequence should be the exercise of proper restraint in making predictions about the future. A recognition of the limits of our human sight is more appropriately Christian in spirit than is dogmatic assertion. If, in the present discussion about hope, Christians show a desire to keep as clear as possible the distinction between what we know and what we don't know, this might well be more convincing evidence to the more sensitive among our contemporaries, both within and outside the churches, of the quality of our hope than dogmatic declaration that fails to acknowledge the ultimate mystery of our life in relation to God.

Our Christian hope is neither dim nor uncertain. It is stronger than death. We live by it and, as Paul says, we are saved by it. But Christian hope is misunderstood unless we see that its deepest characteristic is a trust in God's sovereign love rather than a prescription for what we must do in the times beyond our sight. If we seek to keep our expression of Christian hope anchored in what we do know of God, the nature of that hope becomes clear.

First, love and hope belong together. Our hope is summed up in the expectation that the love we have seen enacted in Jesus Christ will continue to assert itself as the meaning of life (whatever comes), because God is this kind of self-giving, abiding, persuasive love.

God's love is not arbitrary power dazzling us with feats of magic. It is the spirit in which the divine takes upon itself the burden of our human life in its joy and sorrow, its peace and anguish, its living and dying. The resurrection of Jesus Christ means that God has created a new order of life in which everyone may share. Our whole being, past, present, and future, has been brought into a new relationship to God in which there is forgiveness, with the assurance that we share in the victory over everything that threatens community with one another and with God.

Since God has penetrated our humanity with love, we participate here and now in victory over sin and death; for we know that we stand within the circle of a love that is the meaning of all life. When we speak of "realized eschatology" as the theme of the New Testament, this is what we mean. God has made it possible for us to live as those who participate in a love that will assert its ultimate power over all things.

This "realized" new order of life has only begun for us. Christ reigns, but his reign is embattled with the persisting forces that would destroy or threaten the accomplishment of God's purpose. "For he must reign until he has put all his enemies under his feet. The last enemy to be destroyed is death" (1 Cor. 15:25-26). Those who live "in Christ" therefore live as participants in a continuing conflict, yet one in which the crucial victory has been won. Surely this is the Christian experience as we must honestly confess it. Christ remains in conflict with the persistence of lovelessness in us and in the whole order of creation. Yet in the midst of the struggle we live as those who know where its resolution lies.

This knowledge is not something we can demonstrate apart from faith. We know God in the Christian way only when, through God's grace, we have taken up a new stand in relationship to God and to our neighbor. There is no way to understand Christian hope merely by contemplating from outside some propositions about the course of events. We must stand where God's forgiving love meets our loneliness and resentment.[3] But we are saying that the love that can deal with our fears and isolation has been made known to us with power, and that a new life has begun in which we share in God's will for the whole creation.

A second assertion is that God offers us hope for a continuing transformation of our present existence. God works creatively and redemptively in the present to reconstruct our human orders. Therefore, our Christian attitude toward the so-called secular hopes is one both of caution and of positive support. Caution, because the only defensible hopes are those that are consonant with what love requires; positive, because God's will in Christ is to fulfill, not to destroy, our humanity in all its natural and legitimate expression. God knows that we have need of these things, of nourishment and health, of stable justice and peaceful relations, of all the resources that sustain the human body and spirit.

Christian hope, therefore, lends support to every effort to meet human needs. We are obligated as Christians to work within the orders of human life for new good. There have been strong protests in theology against identifying the Kingdom of God with any human program. With this protest we must agree. But if God is as we know the divine in Christ, then it is an equally fatal error to treat creative effort to solve human problems as irrelevant to our salvation.

God has taken time to create the world and life, the human mind and spirit, a time extended beyond our power to imagine. Should we not find meaning in the slow, patient processes of human effort to solve problems of health, justice, and human brotherhood?

The healing of disease takes time, often an agonizing period of waiting and working. Such healing requires planning with the resources of modern knowledge. A determined application of modern medical knowledge cannot be irrelevant to the hope of every Christian who remembers that Jesus practiced healing. Every social good enjoyed in human experience has taken time, planning, and sacrificial human effort. Centuries of political and social struggle went into the attack on slavery, and the struggle must continue. Ages of constitution-making, of revolutionary effort, of legal experience have gone into the securing of whatever freedom to speak and to worship some now enjoy. The spreading of the gospel throughout the world takes time. It takes planning, institutions, and organized technical knowledge as expressions of the missionary spirit.

Time and planning, effort and waiting, experimenting and reconstructing are demands of the world God has given us. To take responsibility in these processes surely brings us closer to a real expression of Christian hope than does disavowal of such effort.

What can we expect from the long struggle with human problems? Probably that it must always go on. Certainly we know that our human contrivances and scientific knowledge are always in part wrongly directed. We cannot pin our Christian hope on any specifiable form of the future of humankind. These are the hard facts of death and destruction. But we believe that the God of the Bible is Lord over creation and history and that we can hope for the meaningful fruition, perhaps in forms we may not now understand, of all efforts to express love and justice in the patient labor of world-building.

The truth in the liberal theologies[4] was the acceptance of this vocation of reconstruction in human affairs as a legitimate expression of Christian hope in history. Certainly this was often put in exaggerated form without a sufficient sense of the tension between our sinful efforts and the full demands of God's righteousness. But when we see that some biblical expressions must be "demythologized" if we are to keep their truth,[5] we might also see that the liberal belief in progress ought to be "demythologized" so that its core of Christian truth may be preserved. That truth is that God works in judgment, in renewal, and in reconstruction in human history, and that therefore no human need should go unrecognized or unmet and no human wrong continue unattacked.

The Content of Christian Hope

The Bible makes some specific statements about future acts of God. It anticipates the second or final coming of Christ. What are we to say of this?

If we speak of the coming of Christ, it is the same Christ who has already come. Therefore his coming must mean that he brings the mystery of God's love and the power of God's judgment. The Christ who once came broke open the meaning of God's love for us so that our sin was exposed, the powers of evil were challenged, and God's will for our renewal was asserted. This came in the strange way of Christ's endurance of the cross.

If we speak now of Christ's coming again, we cannot legitimately mean anything other than that the same judging, cleansing love will assert itself. Reinhold Niebuhr has well reminded us that the Christ who came was not the Christ who was expected. We ought to acknowledge that the Christ who is to come will come in an unexpected way. However he comes, it will be his love bearing our human burden and confronting our sin. This includes the sins of Christians and of the church. It is therefore puzzling, though not uncommon, to hear Christ's coming again spoken of in a jauntily confident mood, as if he were to fulfill all our wishes and set everything right according to our conceptions. But the Christ we know can only come as a further assertion of God's judgment upon us and of love's radical transformation of our existence.

There is one sense in which we can find concrete meaning in Christ's coming again without leaving the realm of identifiable experience. Wherever anyone is brought by experience of life and hearing the gospel to the crisis in which he or she must decide for or against life within the circle of God's love, there that person has met Christ. When out of this crisis the old self-will is broken and the new life has begun, Christ has come again to that person in that place, and the new creation has begun. Such a reinterpretation of Christ's coming again seeks meaning in our present experience for this aspect of the biblical eschatology. Some such reinterpretation seems inevitable for us; indeed, it has already begun in the Fourth Gospel and in Paul's thought.

The final question remains about the coming of Christ as a final act of God bringing an end to history as we know it. What are we to do with these ideas of the Last Judgment, of Christ's coming on clouds in glory with final power (cf. 1 Thess. 4:16-17), of the pictures of eternal life with God in which all tears are wiped away and there is no more sea (Rev. 21:1)? We are creatures who live on the boundary line between time and eternity. Our present experience is qualified in every moment by our dim apprehension that it all moves toward a final accounting. There is acute perception of the importance of this idea in Hannah Arendt's observation arising out of her profound understanding of the development of totalitarianism:

> Nothing perhaps distinguishes modern masses as radically from those of previous centuries as the loss of faith in a Last Judgment: the worst have lost their fear and the best have lost their hope. Unable as yet to live without fear and hope, these masses are attracted by every effort which seems to promise a man-made fabrication of the paradise they have longed for and of the hell they have feared. Just as the popularized features of Marx's classless society have a queer resemblance to the Messianic Age, so the reality of concentration camps resembles nothing so much as medieval pictures of hell.[6]

What Professor Arendt said here of the masses is surely true of every person. We live in the present on the basis of our sense of what ultimately counts. Yet when we try to understand the meaning of "last things" we find grave difficulties. The reason is simply stated: Whenever something is described as an event that ends all events, we are dealing with concepts that defy intelligibility. Events are temporal. They have past, present, and future reference. When we speak of a coming of Christ as an event that ends time, or try to describe resurrection, last judgment, and eternal life, we are making pictures of the unpicturable. What shall we do, then, with these biblical concepts if we are to respect the mystery of ultimate destiny and yet see that in Christian faith we do believe something true and definite about God's sovereignty over all things?

What we can do is to treat the conceptions of the final coming of Christ, of the Last Judgment, as symbolic ideas that occur on the boundary of our knowledge. Since they mark the boundary between what we can know and what we cannot possibly know, they must be recognized as symbols, the specific content of which distorts the very truth they mean to hold. Their actual content for us is the expression they give of our trust in God's righteous judgment and forgiving love as the meaning of all life. We affirm them as expressions of our trust, but in their very nature they remind us that we cannot peer beyond the boundary of the knowledge that is given to us here in this body and in this history.

Since Christian hope is surrounded by the mystery of God's eternal being, we ought not to give our formulations of that hope with partisan cries or dogmatic intolerance; but rather as those who know what it means to be silent before the secret of our faith. As we use theological terms and struggle with strange symbols, we ought not to be intimidated by charges of "theological unintelligibility." The theological language is the language of the Bible and of common speech; but there are no simple means of communicating the themes of redemption and victory over death. We ought to be willing to listen to one another, and above all to the biblical writers, with the humility and restraint appropriate to our finite condition. Acceptance of our limitations, and of our vocation to live in the spirit of love as God's grace makes that possible, will be a more authentic witness to the reality of our hope than partisan clamors or legalistic claims that our version of eschatology is the final one.

5

Tragedy and Hope

The Tragic Vision and
Christian Faith

The issue between Christian faith and the tragic sense of life persists despite all attempts from one side or the other to lay it to rest. In a survey of the literature of the tragic vision, Nathan Scott and Edmond Cherbonnier come to diametrically opposite conclusions. Cherbonnier says that Christian faith is completely opposed to the tragic view. He interprets the tragic outlook as holding that the whole is really good even though it includes both good and evil. He quotes Karl Jaspers's statement that "What is essential to the Christian cannot even emerge in tragedy. . . . Every one of man's basic experiences ceases to be tragic in a Christian context."[1] Jaspers, of course, is highly critical of what he sees as the Christian effort to resolve the problem of evil too simply. But Nathan Scott, in introducing the volume of essays on the tragic visions, says:

> And it is, I feel certain, only those who have accepted a "vocation to tragedy" who can understand the whole point and meaning of Job's declaration, "I know that my redeemer liveth" or who can understand the full poignancy and gloriousness of Paul's word: "If God be for us, who can be against us." Indeed the facts of tragedy are never scanted by the profoundest Christian faith.[2]

Dr. Scott's attempt to mediate between his position and Cherbonnier's seems only to heighten the difference between them.

To meet the issue raised by the tragic vision is one important consideration in interpreting the Christian faith in its eschatological dimension. Does the Christian affirmation of final judgment and eternal
life transcend the tragic perspective, or does it incorporate it, or is it
another version of the tragic outlook? The nature of Christian hope is
at stake, and this chapter is an attempt to consider again the issues
involved.

An initial requirement for the interpretation of Christian eschatology
is the recognition of the many symbols and the variety of affirmations
that make up the Christian expectation. There are symbols of hope and
fulfillment, eternal life, the city without night or tears, the promise that
the faithful will be transformed into the image of Christ (2 Cor. 3:18).
But there is also the history of the lost. In the great judgment in Matthew
25, those on the Lord's right hand will hear the words, "Come, O
blessed of my Father, inherit the kingdom prepared for you from the
foundation of the world" (Matt. 25:34). Those on the left hand who
have not fed or visited or clothed the neighbor will "go away into eternal
punishment." Is this vindication of the divine judgment to be seen as
a tragic victory? And is the failure of those who have not served the
Lord also a failure of God, since they are God's creatures?

Undoubtedly some of the language of the New Testament, especially
that of Paul, can be interpreted as a universal affirmation of salvation.
"For God has consigned all men to disobedience, that he may have
mercy upon all" (Rom. 11:32). At the close of the great passage on
the resurrection in 1 Corinthians 15, which describes the reign of Christ
until he has put all his enemies under his feet, Paul declares that in the
end "God may be everything to every one" (1 Cor. 15:28c). Yet the
New Testament never relaxes the seriousness and ultimacy of the demand
that God lays upon persons, and the necessity of preparation for the
end.

Consider the sense of urgency in the second letter of Peter with its
vision of the present earth:

> But do not ignore this one fact, beloved, that with the Lord one day
> is as a thousand years, and a thousand years as one day. The Lord is
> not slow about his promise as some count slowness, but is forbearing
> toward you, not wishing that any should perish, but that all should
> reach repentance. But the day of the Lord will come like a thief, and
> then the heavens will pass away with a loud noise, and the elements
> will be dissolved with fire, and the earth and the works that are upon
> it will be burned up.

> Since all these things are thus to be dissolved, what sort of persons
> ought you to be in lives of holiness and godliness, waiting for and
> hastening the coming of the day of God, because of which the heavens
> will be kindled and dissolved, and the elements will melt with fire!
> But according to his promise we wait for new heavens and a new
> earth in which righteousness dwells. (2 Peter 3:8-10, 13)

The words of ultimate hope are here, but the new heaven and the
new earth come after the fiery tragedy of the old. The demand for
watchful waiting comes with the fully serious warning of the possibility
of being unprepared. Does this mean that those who meet the end
without faith are truly lost? Is man's response to God only a matter of
hastening the coming of the day of the Lord, or is it a decision that
involves blessedness for some and destruction for others? Such questions
persist through the history of Christian interpretation of the last things.
They appear in the background of James Russell Lowell's hymn:

> Careless seems the great Avenger; history's ages record
> One death-grapple in the darkness 'twixt old systems and the Word:
> Truth forever on the scaffold, Wrong forever on the throne,
> Yet the scaffold sways the future, and behind the dim unknown
> Standeth God within the shadow, keeping watch above his own.[3]

The Christian hymnodists have felt it desirable to alter Lowell's line,
"Wrong forever on the throne," as inconsistent with the Christian faith,
so that the version usually sung goes, "And upon the throne be wrong."
But is Lowell's original version not closer to one strand of Christian
eschatology? So long as this earth's history goes on, there is a persistent
mystery of evil. And while God keeps watch "above his own," does this
mean over some or over all? Is history tragic in the sense that there is
a partial frustration of the divine purpose; or is the loss of some life,
the presence of unrelieved evil, a part of the divine purpose? If there is
real evil, can we speak of its overcoming as tragic, or must we speak of
it in some other way in order to see history from the standpoint of the
redemptive power of God? Such questions, of course, take us to the
final mysteries. We are not given simple answers with which we can
predict the literal outcome of history. We are dealing with the nature
of our faith itself, and the experience of redemption that underlies it.
What does the Christian faith see in the conflict of good and evil in
history?

The Nature of the Tragic Resolution

In order to deal with the problem of Christianity and tragedy, we have to face the complex question of what we mean by the tragic. In the book already referred to, Nathan Scott says quite rightly that a broad definition of tragedy is required if justice is to be done to the many forms of expression that must somehow be recognized as holding a tragic element. He defines the tragic as "an *attitude* of *attentiveness* to the contingencies and sufferings that it is the lot of man to endure."[4]

Scott shifts the attention here from any particular worldview, or any special doctrine of the tragic resolution, to the attitude of the beholder of suffering. While I agree about the necessity of this broad definition of tragedy, one qualification must be added; namely, that the beholder finds some meaning or truth revealed and established in the experience of beholding suffering—a meaning or truth by which in some sense the evil becomes, if not endurable, at least a source of some meaningful response in the beholder.

This is necessary to distinguish the tragic outlook from sheer defeat or cynicism. It is not attentiveness in itself, but the wresting of some meaning out of the wasteland of life, that marks the tragic attitude. It may be the meaning of sheer defiance of ineluctable fate, as in Bertrand Russell's *A Free Man's Worship,* or a wistful waiting for something that is utterly beyond shape or hope, as in Samuel Beckett's *Waiting for Godot,* but there is some significant ordered response in man in the presence of the agony and the failure that endows the whole with meaning.

Because the experience of evil is so varied, and because the kind of meaning that is taken from it shifts from age to age, culture to culture, and person to person, the meaning of the "tragic" stretches over a wide range of human experience. It is necessary, therefore, if we are to interpret Christian hope in relation to the tragic outlook in the twentieth century, to take account of two particularly important forms of the existence of evil.

It is characteristic of the tragic literature of the twentieth century that attention shifts from the man of heroic stature in whom a fatal flaw is discovered, often at the point of his very strength and greatness, to the "little man" who is buffeted by powers that he cannot withstand and does not understand. In classic Greek tragedy and in Shakespearean tragedy, the hero comes to know what his or her fate is and what powers determine it. Oedipus discovers what he has done and knows that he has incurred the inescapable penalty. There is dignity and heroic stature in his resignation to the consequences of his deeds. Macbeth's discovery that through his act life has come to be a "tale told by an idiot, full of sound and fury, signifying nothing" is the denouement of his own moral failure. He himself has destroyed the possibility of meaning that life once held.

In contemporary tragedy the theme is much more likely to be that of the senseless waste and destruction of human life by the ruthless forces of nature and society. It is the little person who emerges as the tragic figure, the one for whom no overall structure of interpretation of life is given or is possible, and whose fate it is to be beaten down and to die without knowing what any of it really means. That figure is found, for example, in the soldier Wozzeck in Alban Berg's opera of that name, in some of William Faulkner's characters, and in Arthur Miller's salesman Willy Loman.

In a comment on the theme of *Death of a Salesman,* the distinguished drama critic Brooks Atkinson noted the tragic dimensions of the play. He received a number of protests against describing it as tragic. One protestor summed up his reaction by saying of Willy Loman, "He is a pathetic, not a tragic figure who we can neither pity nor admire." Atkinson's reply is worth noting, for it has implications that put the contemporary experience of tragedy in the right perspective:

> It would be either arrogant or pedantic to deny the dignity of tragedy to the millions of obscure people who have died for causes in which they believed or in circumstances they could not control. . . . Because the common man is anonymous it is easy to be supercilious about him. . . . The classic definition of tragedy is too narrow to have much practical validity. For the common man can suffer too, and those whom he loves can grieve. As Willy Loman's widow said, "Attention must be paid." Tragedy is the common experience.[5]

There is meaning in the tragic experience as the dramatist sees it, if only the meaning of calling attention to the suffering and the refusal to be unconcerned. Because the heroic resignation and insight into the ways of the moral order are not always available to the contemporary person in our depersonalized world, tragedy takes on a new dimension, and its resolution must be of a different kind. A double demand is placed here on a theology that speaks to this situation: It must deal with the question of the "unconcerned" universe, and it must ask in what sense the Christian resolution of the tragic plight may assert its relevance to the situation of the person who can neither see nor believe in a moral order in which all lives have their rightful destinies as exemplifying an ultimate principle of truth or courage.

To this situation of the common person searching for some meaning in existence, we must add a further dimension before we can see the full impact of the problem of tragedy in our time. This dimension is the fact of mass destruction of life. This is not simply the fate of the lone individual, but the fate of peoples and civilizations, which raises the ultimate question about the meaning of human existence in a way that must be faced by Christian interpretation of the eschatological hope.

To be sure, mass destruction is nothing new in human experience. The slaughter of six million Jews by the Nazis is one more chapter in the incredible story of the destruction of whole populations, as recounted in the Old Testament itself and in every history of human cultures. Nature is a destroyer. Volcanic eruptions have blotted out cities, and disease and drought have ended civilizations. The New Testament affirmation that not a sparrow falls to the ground outside the knowing and providential care of God has always been asserted in the face of these facts. Yet there really is a new element in our time in the possible mass destruction through calculated technical proficiency and nuclear weapons.

It might be said that war of mass destruction reinforces a moral view of humanity's tragic situation because it is humanity that develops the weapons, controls them, and who would be responsible for the resulting holocaust. To this, however, it must be said that in some respects the weapons of mass destruction have increased the contemporary person's view of the senselessness of threatening forces. The release of the technical powers of destruction is not necessarily decided by any one individual or any one responsible group. It may be a function of the forces and conflicts in which people are caught. The war that might end the human enterprise on this planet might not be the result of any human will to have such a war; but rather of the collective fears and insecurities of nations—even, it now appears, of a miscalculation and accidental touching off of the final catastrophe.

This is not to say there is no place for human responsibility and decision in the meeting of the historical crisis of our time; but only to uncover one source of the contemporary person's feeling that whatever happens, he or she is dealing with unmanageable forces that treat human life as something dispensable.

It is worth observing that wherever the sense of human helplessness before such forces evokes a real concern and therefore causes some kind of protest, a new meaning for human existence is pressing for recognition.[6] We have said that tragedy always involves an implicit evaluation of life and a search for some point of reference by which evil can be judged. Unless life is of some worth, its destruction is no more a problem than is its creation. It is fair to say, then, that the increasing modern sense of an ultimate problem in the fate of the helpless individual, or in the helpless mass of mankind in the midst of destructive forces, is in part the result of the higher valuation of the worth of each person and the heightened concern about the lowliest and most helpless individual that Christianity more than any other source has brought into human history.

When drama critic Atkinson insists on the right of the common person to the dignity of tragic experience, he is reiterating a theme that has its roots in the New Testament concern with "the least of these." And when Albert Camus in his Nobel prize acceptance declares his refusal to be reconciled to a universe in which innocent children suffer, and says that the creative artist will not "serve the armies of tyranny" but will heed the silence of the "unknown prisoner," he is viewing the problem of tragic existence at the precise point where Christian faith has tried to meet it. The ultimate significance of every life is affirmed in the face of the world's evil. The problem of Christian eschatology is to show in what sense the symbols of judgment, resurrection, and eternal life can express a genuine hope without glossing over the realities of experience. Camus protests that Christian faith has solved the problem too easily by affirming a reconciliation and fulfillment in some transcendent realm.

> There is an evil, undoubtedly, which men accumulate in their frantic desire for unity. But yet another evil lies at the roots of this inordinate movement. Confronted with this evil, confronted with death, man from the very depths of his soul cries out for justice. Historical Christianity has only replied to this protest against evil by the annunciation of the kingdom and then of eternal life, which demands faith. But suffering exhausts hope and faith and then is left alone and unexplained. The toiling masses, worn out with suffering and death, are masses without God. Our place is henceforth at their side, far from teachers, old or new. Historical Christianity postpones to a point beyond the span of history the cure of evil and murder, which are nevertheless experienced within the span of history.[7]

If this is the outcome of Christian doctrine, we shall have to accept an unreconcilable break between the tragic sense of contemporary man and the Christian faith. But I do not believe this is the outcome. There are two aspects of Christian eschatology and they must be taken together, for neither by itself expresses the full meaning of the Christian expectation regarding God's overcoming of evil.

The Meaning of the
Eschatological Symbols

Before we come to the analysis of these two dimensions of Christian eschatology, we must face the question of meaning and the criterion of assertions about the last things, for the eschatological symbols point beyond all present experience and all possible history to a final disclosure of the will and power of God.

The problem, therefore, of making a responsible use of the eschatological symbols is a serious one. We are speaking beyond our sight and beyond our competence about ultimate matters. Human wishes, hopes, resentments, fears, and faiths have a wide range of expression in thoughts about the future, eternal life, and ultimate destiny. We must use some criteria of relevance and truth in speaking of the eschatological dimension, otherwise it is simply affirmation without support. Shall the biblical symbols be interpreted, as Rudolf Bultmann suggests, by seeking an existential base through which they can be translated into terms that coincide with our self-understanding in the light of the new and absolute offering in the gospel? Or shall they be regarded as necessary but symbolic anticipations of the destiny that is implied in the gospel but transcends all self-understanding?

Without attempting to enter here into all the methodological problems involved, I shall make three brief statements about the meaning and truth of the eschatological assertions.

1. The first point is a descriptive one. There is a wealth of eschatological symbols in the Scripture, and they appear not in systematic order but in a profusion of unsystematized expression. The resurrection of the body, eternal life, heaven and hell, the return of the Lord, the final conflict with Antichrist, the new heavens and the new earth—all these appear as expressions of the Christian understanding of ultimate things, but they cannot be brought into a simple logical order, nor can they all be shown to derive with equal clarity and necessity from the central theme of the gospel. In his study of Jesus, *The Kingdom of God and the Son of Man,* Rudolph Otto points out the characteristic of all apocalyptic: its wealth of symbols, their paradoxical character, the impossibility of bringing them into a logically consistent order. We can take them as

significant expressions of the way in which the gospel leads us to look to the future without making literal systematic assertions out of them.

2. The eschatological symbols have roots in experience, and we are able to give them meaning insofar as we discover what ground they have in our knowledge of God's redemptive action. We can speak about the return of the Lord because the Word has already become flesh and dwelt among us. We can begin to grasp the meaning of life eternal, because it is already disclosed to us in the knowledge of God given in the gospel (John 17:3). We can assert the reality of final judgment because there is a present, authentic experience of the judgment of God in history and in personal existence.

Eschatology is an anticipation of last things on the basis of the self-revelation of God's ultimate will and character in actual history.

3. My third remark concerns a special aspect of at least some of the eschatological statements and symbols in the New Testament. They carry a warning against our claiming an absolute knowledge of the end. Jesus' declaration that "But of that day or hour no one knows, not even the angels in heaven, nor the Son, but only the Father" (Mark 13:32) and his rebukes of those who demand a sign of the kingdom are permanent warnings against an eschatology that does not accept the limits of human knowledge. Paul returns many times to the same theme, "Now we see in a mirror dimly, but then face to face" (1 Cor. 13:12). And Paul's expressions concerning the resurrection carry reminders of the mystery. "Lo! I tell you a mystery. We shall not all sleep, but we shall all be changed, in a moment, in the twinkling of an eye, at the last trumpet" (1 Cor. 15:51-52). One of his most important images is found in his assertion that at the end we shall know as we are known (1 Cor. 13:12). A clear distinction between God's knowledge and ours is the first requirement of Christian wisdom.

How then shall we understand the biblical eschatology? Let us assert the general principle that the eschatological symbols form a cluster of expressions of Christian expectation and hope that have to be taken together, not as a system but as a series of symbols that are meaningful for us insofar as we can see in them expressions of the Christian understanding of God and God's ways with persons, rooted in the revelation in Jesus Christ. They do not refer simply to present experience. They are anticipations of the future, assertions about ultimate and final things, but their meaning lies in the validity with which they grow out of the knowledge of God, God's judgment and redemptive purpose and God's saving power manifest in the history of dealing with human persons as we grasp and understand that history in the Christian faith.

We can freely accept the symbolic character of eschatological assertions. We can refuse to make all fit together in a single scheme. We can
take them as significant expressions of a dimension of the Christian
faith that looks toward the last things on the basis of the reconciliation
that God has accomplished in Jesus Christ and that he will continue
"until [Christ] has put all his enemies under his feet" (1 Cor. 15:25).

The Tragic Theme in the History
of Redemption

Tragedy results from the conflict of good with evil. Some real good is
at stake in the conflict, and some real threat to that good exists. We are
asking how Christian eschatology interprets the conflict of God's will
with the evil in humanity and in the cosmos. The first point to be made
is that the conflict is recognized as real, and in the New Testament is
the final judgment in which all that has opposed God's purpose will be
exposed, defeated, and consigned to its proper "place," outer darkness
or total destruction. It will not participate in the life of the kingdom.
Matthew's Gospel records the warning of Jesus:

> Whoever receives one such child in my name receives me; but whoever
> causes one of these little ones who believe in me to sin, it would be
> better for him to have a great millstone fastened round his neck and
> be drowned in the depth of the sea.
>   Woe to the world for temptations to sin. For it is necessary that
> temptations come, but woe to the man by whom the temptation comes.
> (Matt. 18:5-7)

The charge that the Christian faith allows us to be reconciled to the
sufferings of the innocent can certainly be refuted in the light of such
statements. It is true that this does not meet fully the objection of Camus
and those who stand with him that suffering for the innocent comes
not only from the wrongdoing of persons, but from conditions in nature
and life for which no one is responsible. That issue must be met in any
interpretation of Christian eschatology. At this point it may be observed
that the New Testament faith calls for an active concern about all human
needs. It combines the injunction not to be anxious for the morrow
with the command to feed the hungry and clothe the naked. There is
no exemption from responsible concern for and ministry to human
needs.
  No argument of a theodicy type appears in the New Testament. There
is no attempt to prove that the world is really better the way it is than

any other possible way. Paul's statement that God has "consigned all men to disobedience, that he may have mercy upon all" (Rom. 11:32) might be an exception, but even it does not demonstrate that all is for the best. Such arguments, of course, have been made. There is George Santayana's jibe at fellow philosopher Josiah Royce, who, Santayana says, held that it was absolutely right that things should be wrong, and absolutely wrong not to try to set them right.[8] Royce did argue in this way, though never in those words, and he was following the line of the theodicies of Augustine, Calvin, and Leibnitz, all of whom felt it necessary to show that things ought to be as they are.

But such arguments are not part of the Christian faith or necessary to it. To believe in God is indeed to believe that it is right there should be a world that includes life, growth, and real freedom. Within the purpose of God we are offered such a life so that we may participate freely in the divine purpose and look toward fulfillment in a kingdom of loving and creative relationships. It is within the meaning of God's goodness and providence that there should be such a world. But all our experience tells us that it is a world in which there is struggle and risk. If freedom is real, then it is the freedom of the creatures to direct their lives in some measure as they will, and therefore it is freedom to create disorder where there ought to be order, and to be self-seeking where they ought to be seeking the kingdom of God.

In this view, conflict between God and the creatures is possible. It is a conflict whose ultimate terms are set by God, not by the creatures. The will to be free of God and the consequences of divine law cannot succeed. But within the boundaries set by God there is a real history of God's contention with humanity. It begins in the story of creation and carries through the history of Israel. It rises to its climax in the conflict of Jesus with "his own." Christ weeps over Jerusalem: "O Jerusalem, Jerusalem, killing the prophets and stoning those who are sent to you! How often would I have gathered your children together as a hen gathers her brood under her wings, and you would not!" (Luke 13:34). Here is the divine longing and the failure of the human response. This is tragedy surely, that humanity should be created for peace and joy in the kingdom of God and should turn away from it. The Scripture is filled with such descriptions of history in which the possibility of life's fulfillment in God's order is missed. There is the young man who turns away sadly from Jesus "for he had great possessions" (Mark 10:22). Two thieves are crucified with the Lord; one reviles him, the other finds saving faith (Luke 23:39-40). This is the tragic theme in its Christian context.

Once the moments of decision are gone, they do not return. Whatever may be done later to repair or renew the damage people do to themselves and their fellows, the hour of unfaith and hatred is the hour of tragic loss. The moral seriousness of the gospel cannot be interpreted otherwise. Good may be brought out of evil. New possibilities are opened up in the depths of the tragic experience, but these do not set aside or cancel the element of real loss in the tragic failure of human beings.

But in what sense is the loss irretrievable? It may be said that God's redemptive activity takes the loss up into a new structure of meaning that does not cancel it but uses it. This is the Christian hope. But is everything "saved"? We come here to the issue of universalism in the Christian faith, and it must be said that the issue has never been resolved in Christian thinking. The traditional symbols of heaven and hell seem to present the possibility of fulfillment for some, lostness for others. They are difficult symbols, partly because they are not given extensive development in the Scripture, and partly because they have been subjected to so much interpretation that betrays the continuing self-centeredness and vindictiveness of people more than it does the love of God affirmed in the gospel.

There are also universalistic sayings in the New Testament that can be used to support the view that in the end none will be lost. God is sovereign, and since God loves, God must will the redemption of all.[9]

While we are dealing here with matters that remain necessarily far beyond our sight and competence, we must take seriously the main weight of the Christian interpretation of the meaning of God's contention with humankind and say that it is possible for persons to lose their share in the kingdom. It is not necessary to paint the picture of hell as a place of divine vengeance or endless suffering, which would be pointless; but only to recognize that the hell of separation from God, which is also separation from oneself and separation from one's neighbor, is a genuine risk in our freedom. Here we can speak existentially, not speculatively. The literature of our time has pictured the real hells of experience as vividly as did Dante or Jonathan Edwards. Consider Sartre's *No Exit* or Albert Camus's *The Fall*.[10]

Christian faith has never regarded the fate of the lost as meaningless. It exhibits the justice of God that is vindicated in every destiny, and in this sense we may speak of God's victory as always accomplished. But on the question of how we are to understand the divine intention in the face of the fact that some actually will themselves into the hell of self-isolation, Christian theology has wavered. Strict predestinarian doctrines hold that all is determined from the beginning and every destiny flows from the single will of God. Theologies that have found the consequences of this doctrine intolerable have qualified it. Karl Barth seems close to a universalistic doctrine of salvation, showing how far the revolt against the tradition has gone within Reformed theology itself.[11]

Either we have to assert the universalist doctrine that all are ultimately saved, or we have to accept a tragic element in the loss of the meaning and fulfillment of life by those who in their freedom resist the offer of God. The meaning of tragedy here is partly that there is real loss, the waste of possibilities. But there is also a positive meaning to be found in this tragic experience, and Christian faith has not overlooked it. It is the disclosure of the depths of the seriousness of life, and the vindication of the divine order. God is not mocked. The refusal to love leads to the loss of the good life. The systems of injustice produce the forces that overthrow them. The idols are exposed and leave people who have worshiped them with the emptiness of a shattered confidence. "Their feet are swift to shed blood, in their paths are ruin and misery, and the way of peace they do not know" (Rom. 3:15-17).

The meaning derived from the tragic picture of the lost in the New Testament is not so much a purgation as a warning. The destiny of the unrighteous is an occasion for hearing again the promise of the kingdom to those who repent. It is a reminder that no one lives without the grace of God; for all have sinned and all have come short. There is then a participation in tragedy with a possibility of using the knowledge of evil and its consequence for an overcoming of evil. In the universal history of humankind, a divine justice is manifest that in the end will apportion all the consequences in such a way that the sense of the whole can be seen. Christian theology that accepts the risks of moral freedom must acknowledge a tragic dimension in God's dealings with human beings in history.

The Tragic Element in Natural Evil

Thus far we have spoken of tragedy in moral terms. We have yet to meet the issue of the loss, waste, suffering, and destruction that human life experiences through the course of nature, the accidents of history, the passage of time that makes wreckage out of every human creation.

Once we admit the reality of natural evil, a grave question arises for Christian faith and indeed for any meaningful reconciliation of persons with existence. Must we not account as tragic the way in which nature wastes the human potential—as, for example, in starvation and disease that cut the life span and may brutalize persons in their scramble for survival? Beyond every element of cruelty, unnecessary suffering, and inhumanity committed by people, there is still the mystery of evil in nature. Does the Christian faith lead to a simple reconciliation with this, or does it accept a tragic element in nature, one that must be met with a spirit that finds meaning in the tragedy?

Christian piety has always sought some spiritual gain in the bearing of the pains of life. "The Lord disciplines him whom he loves" (Heb. 12:6). Paul says suffering produces endurance, and endurance character, and character hope (Rom. 5:3). This much can be validated in experience: that the human person finds courage, moral stature, and capacity for hope in a world filled with risks and natural evils. Theology can neither explain away natural evil nor treat it as sheer misery without shedding any light on its meaning. We have to be careful about saying what is evil in nature and what is not. Disease leads to the loss of precious life, but the struggle for existence is part of life's structure. Who has the wisdom to say it should be otherwise?

This caution, however, does not allow us to deny the tragic element. We know there are evils that result from the ways of nature. The question is whether Christian faith finds some common ground with the tragic outlook in trying to wrest a meaning out of this evil. There is no reason to reject the discovery that the facing of such evil can lead humankind to spiritual insight. Santayana speaks of the possibility that "there may be words, there may be hard facts, there may be dark abysses before which intelligence must be silent for fear of going mad." He finds meaning even in this, for we can "entrench ourselves impregnably in our insignificance. The very act of recognizing our insignificance, if sincere and not a mask for new claims, removes the sting of that insignificance."[12]

The Christian might not use exactly the same terms but can certainly agree that the lesson of a person's "insignificance" before the power of the Creator has entered into the substance of Christian faith from the Eighth Psalm and the Book of Job throughout the whole of Christian experience. Paul Tillich accepts the tragic element in nature-history, and points out that there can be no absolute separation between the evil in nature and the sin in man. "Man reaches into nature, as nature reaches into man. . . . This makes it possible and necessary to use the term 'fallen world' and to apply the concept of existence (in contrast to essence) to the universe as well as to man. . . ."[13] If the Christian and the person who lives by the tragic outlook find themselves close together, it is because they have looked at the same realities and have found a meaning in humanity's honest and undefeated acceptance of the conditions of mortal existence.

While this tragic theme is not set aside in Christian experience, it is not the last word. We have now to see how the eschatological hope moves beyond the tragic perspective without denying it.

The Transmutation of Tragedy

The key to the Christian transmutation of the tragic outlook lies in the faith in God's redemptive action as involving resources for overcoming evil in an ultimate fulfillment. But it is important to emphasize the aspect of the divine resources, not the prediction of the outcome. It is here that an eschatology that remains true to the limits of our sight will differ from one that seeks to make predictions about the final disposal of every evil. If the Christian hope for redemption involves the assurance that every evil will be made good, then Camus's criticism of Christianity seems valid: It is impossible to take seriously the actual struggle with evil in history, for it changes nothing. All will be well in the end anyhow.

The Christian hope, however, can be given a different interpretation. We know that divine action can transform present evil into future good, that forgiveness can heal the evil in the spirit, that a new community is possible when the old is broken. All life, therefore, participates in a history whose full meaning is not known until the whole is accomplished. It is here that the symbols of resurrection, final judgment, and eternal life become necessary expressions of the hope by which the Christian lives. They are not predictions of the outcome, but assertions, reminders, and symbols of the fact that life exists in an unfinished history whose final meaning depends upon the ultimate resources of God. No life is finished until its history is finished, and each life history is bound up with the history of the whole.

Here we may have some light on the problem of the meaning of that great variety or inequality of opportunities for spiritual growth that exists in the human pilgrimage. A child beaten and rejected by a mentally sick parent may not have the opportunity to know the love of God as might the child in a loving home. Persons' souls are shaped by the religious cultures in which they live. Idolatry, superstition, insight, moralism, spirituality, and faith all come to us embodied in particular forms and traditions. No one can say God's self-revelation is simply spread out for all to see in the same profound and adequate way. And if one lives in a complacent Christendom, this may be, as Kierkegaard saw it, not so much a privilege of being close to the gospel as an almost insurmountable barrier to hearing what the gospel really is.

What is the Christian understanding of this vast complexity of the human pilgrimage, especially since Christianity sees the personal disclosure of God as given to one people in one strand of history, in a way it has not been given elsewhere?

The Christian answer lies in the conception of a history of redemption in which each creature participates in the possibilities, the limitations, the struggle with evil, and the birth of hope that is possible for each. Nor should we say that in the Christian community we *have* salvation, while others only *participate* in it. All participate, all live a history that is not finished, all may look forward to a consummation not yet given, all must acknowledge the ultimate boundaries of our sight beyond which lies the destiny prepared by God. The eschatological symbols, filled as they are with hope for both divine judgment and for salvation, take on their special character as anticipations of the victory of God without denying the actuality and seriousness of the struggle between good and evil in history and in every life. The direction of hope is toward the future, but the basis of hope is in the past and present.

The roots of eschatology lie in the discernment of redemptive possibilities already disclosed. There are two major aspects of this grounding of the Christian hope, which we may note in conclusion.

The first basis of eschatological hope is the reality of forgiveness, disclosed decisively in Jesus Christ and appropriated in faith. It is important to note that the experience of forgiveness, which leads the Christian to hope for a reconciliation in the darkest depths of human existence, is not founded on an experience of perfect consummation of a new life in which sin is eliminated; but rather on the disclosure that the beginning of a new life beyond the destructiveness of sin is possible. Eschatologically this means that the resources of the divine mercy cannot be ruled out of any future or out of any life. It rejects the doctrine that God consigns any soul to an irrevocable hell. There may be irrevocable hells to which people in their freedom drive themselves; but they are irrevocable because of what people decided, not because of the will of a merciful God. There is no basis in faith or experience for concluding that every soul will finally know the peace and joy of life with God; but there is the basis in Christian experience for asserting that in the face of any evil and sin in the human spirit, there is always the power of the divine mercy as our ultimate resource. The meaning of any life is not given finally until that resource has been fully explored. We live into a future we cannot see, but we know that God is in it.

The second Christian affirmation has to do with the divine possibility of using the evil of life to serve new good. It is true that God makes "the wrath of men" to praise God (Ps. 76:10). Certainly there is much evil in human life for which we can see no possible use, now or in the future. I have taken the position here that the Christian faith does not require us to say that every evil is redeemable and must necessarily be brought into some service to the divine purpose.[14] But what we must not overlook in the Christian understanding of evil is that there are ways in which evil is turned against itself. The supreme example is the way in which the hatred of people against the Christ who brings the love and truth of God into history is turned into the occasion of the supreme manifestation of that love on the cross. Here is the disclosure of a new possibility that stands within every situation, a possibility of a redemptive history in which this present will be transformed, its meaning transfigured, and its evil (which is really evil) made to serve the good.

In this view we have moved beyond the tragic perspective as final, for in tragedy the meaning of life must be found without any ultimate hope of restoration, forgiveness, or transfiguration. Thus, the Christian can accept the tragic dimension without being confined to it.

It may be objected that this view is a compromise within the traditional terms of eschatology. Instead of asserting absolutely what disposal will be made of evil, it points to what might be. But is a reliance upon what "might come to be" enough ground for hope? I have met this objection in part by stressing that the ground of the hope for what might be is to be found in the Christian experience of what is. Eschatology is an anticipation of the ultimate use of the divine resources in the way in which we know they are manifest in the evil in us and around us.

There is a sense in which this "might be" is accepted in this view, for what is involved is the reality of freedom. To take seriously the freedom of God is to refuse to limit the form of Christian hope to the tragic perspective; for God has freedom to restore and renew beyond the tragic resolution. But to take seriously the freedom of the creatures, and especially the freedom of humanity, is to accept an element of real venture and risk in the story of God's redemptive action. God wills a kingdom for all, but since it is the kingdom of the spirit, God will have it on no other terms than persons' free decision and response. Thus, we can live with an unquenchable hope without denying the seriousness of human decisions, and without making premature peace with any evil on the ground that it ultimately can be made into good.

6

Love, Death, and Hope

Process and Hope

Our aim in this chapter is to show how the doctrine of love can con-
tribute to a theology of hope. Love and hope are bound together in
life and in the Christian faith. It is love that is the root of hope, not
hope the root of love. Love gives the criterion for judging the forms
of hope, even while love feeds upon hope, for love requires freedom
to venture into the future.

The theologies of hope developed by Jürgen Moltmann, Johannes
Metz, Wolfhart Pannenberg, and others have helped Christian theology
recover significant dimensions of the gospel. They have been especially
powerful in stressing the biblical theme of the solidarity of humanity
and the collective character of the hope for the Kingdom of God. With
Ernst Bloch's powerful social philosophy of hope in the background,
the theologies of hope are also influenced by biblical prophetism, Marx-
ism, and the pietism of the radical sectarians stemming from Thomas
Müntzer. This ecstatic and revolutionary expectation has appeared con-
sistently throughout Christian history. It has been combined with an
exegesis of the prophetic hope in the Bible and often with the apocalyptic
outlook.

Some theologies of hope concentrated so much on the future and on
God's promise that the question of the roots of hope has been somewhat
obscured. The relation between the expected future and present action
has not been clarified, and the New Testament's central theme of the
new relationship between humanity and God created in Jesus Christ

has been oversimplified. It is to these issues that a theology of hope today must address itself.

Process theologies have always been theologies of hope. I shall try to show how the interpretation of Christian faith in the perspective of the process doctrine can face the issues of death and hope, and the promise of earthly peace and justice, so as to deal fairly with both the presence and the promise of God's action in history. We are dealing with a many-sided theme; for the forms of hope can be as varied and as novel in history as the forms of love, and for the same reason. They both stem from the creative action of God in freedom evoking the free response of creatures in a real history.[1]

I will defend two main theses here. The first is that love is the ground of hope. God is not only future; God is the creator present in every moment of past and present as redemptive love. We can hope because we have grasped something, however fragmentarily, of the meaning of life in a community of mutual concern. In process theology, to become is to hope. In every act of becoming we lay hold of future possibility. All creative response is initiated in a subjective aim that moves toward the future. But the aim at being must reach some fulfillment in every pulsation of life, or else existence would be nothing. We seek to become here and now in such a way that present possibility is realized and future possibility is opened. I state this general metaphysical principle because metaphysics can serve as an instrument of insight into the concrete realities of the Christian faith. It is through the presence of God that the promise of God is known.

The second main thesis is that love transforms both the mode and the content of our hoping. Hopes are distorted when love is self-centered or self-destructive. Love always hopes, but as love discovers its real meaning, we hope in such a way that the future is faced without fear and without the demand for knowing how it will turn out. Love in the Christian sense, I shall argue, does not demand to know the completion of its hopes; it demands participation in an infinite creativity where hope will always be a dimension of free creative life. Love learns to accept the risks and openness of the future, and in that acceptance love becomes stronger to face those risks. Loving hope is not a demand upon God to fulfill our wishes for ourselves or for the world. Loving hope is the will to entrust this present, and all times, to God.

These theses raise some issues in regard to the way in which death and resurrection, earthly hopes and the Kingdom of God, have been traditionally viewed. Part of our difficulty is that there are several biblical eschatologies, just as there are several biblical christologies. It is not a matter of finding the one biblical outlook, but of reflecting within faith on the central tendencies of the Scriptures. It is not possible here to review all the biblical material. I shall offer an interpretation with some illustrative texts. We are searching for a fundamental perspective within which we may view the relationship of faith, hope, and love biblically understood. The point I shall argue for is one most traditional eschatologies have obscured, because they have been insistent on knowing the shape of the future and too little willing to leave the future open to God's free dealing with people.

Presence and Promise in the Scriptures

The Bible recognizes many dimensions of hope. Life depends on the fulfillment of hope for daily bread, for health and healing, for success in the ventures that sustain us. We live by collective hopes for our communities, nations, peace in the world, and the advancement of human knowledge and skill. The Bible affirms earthly hopes. Even the New Testament, with all its apocalyptic expectation, affirms earthly needs. Jesus says, "Seek first the Kingdom of God and all these things will be added" (Matt. 6:33). The apocalyptic picture of the end includes the chiliastic expectation of the thousand-year reign of peace, a hope that echoes the Old Testament visions of earthly peace with swords beaten into ploughshares. This chiliastic expectation has played an important role in the revolutionary hopes for a new order in history, expressed in Christian forms of utopianism.

In all dimensions of hope, the biblical outlook sees its ground as an experience of God's faithful, redemptive power and love. The expectation in the prophetic faith is grounded in trust in the God who is loyal to creation and to us, and who can be depended upon for both judgment and mercy. Certainly God can and will create a new order, a new covenant, a new heaven and earth, but this is said hopefully because God's self-revelation is faithful and loving.

The Old Testament, for all its theme of promise, offers a powerful counterpoint in the affirmation of God's presence. The opening of the second Isaiah's prophecy is in this mode:

> Comfort, comfort my people,
>   says your God,
> Speak tenderly to Jerusalem,
>   and cry unto her

that her warfare is ended,
  her iniquity is pardoned. (Isa. 40:1-2)

The figure of the Suffering Servant is a bearer of reconciliation in history, the witness of God's faithfulness and the sign of redemption. The promise is to him and those he represents:

The will of the Lord shall prosper in his hand;
he shall see the fruit of the travail of his soul
  and be satisfied. (Isa. 53:10-11)

The expectancy in the Old Testament is rarely expressed as a sheer reliance on promise; it is expectancy born of a present realization of God's will and power.

For the mountains may depart
  and the hills be removed,
But my steadfast love shall not depart from you,
  And my covenant of peace shall not be removed,
  says the Lord. (Isa. 54:10)

God's presence and promise are mutual implicates. The same faithful love that is the ground of trust in God gives the content of the promised reign of righteous love.

Yet the Day of God is postponed. The reign of peace does not arrive. The wars for the land continue and Israel is under the Roman yoke. It is in this period before the New Testament that the form of prophetic expectation becomes apocalyptic. Now the theme of resurrection begins to play a larger role in the form of hope, whereas before the horizon of hope was largely confined to this world, and death led only to a shadowy *sheol*.

In the New Testament this mutual relationship between presence and promise remains in the form of hope; but there is a new structure in the understanding of time and history because in Jesus, Messiah has come. He is the center of history from which both past and future are newly understood. In him, God has inaugurated a new history. He is the vine, his people the branches. Believing in him is participation in eternal life.

This Johannine theme appears also throughout Paul's letters. "You have died, and your life is hid with Christ in God" (Col. 3:3). So freedom is not simply promised, it is given. "For freedom Christ has set us free; stand fast therefore, and do not submit again to a yoke of slavery" (Gal. 5:1). The Spirit that is the Spirit of God disclosed in Jesus is present reality and present power. "Walk by the Spirit" (Gal. 5:16).

Yet hope must remain. The mystery of death, the conflict of divine righteousness and human sin go on. The characteristic theme of the New Testament is that we live by hope but now *within* the new reality that God has created in Christ. Indeed there is still a "not yet." Satan the enemy still prowls. Further, we know that the life of faith carries no guarantee against our losing the vital center of this relationship. Paul pleads with the Galatians not to be entangled again in the yoke of bondage. The pastoral epistles are full of warnings of judgment.

Thus the entire structure of apocalyptic eschatology is kept and at some points elaborated, especially in the teaching of Jesus recorded in the Synoptics and in the Revelation of John. The church lives in the expectation of the "end"; but believing people still live in the world of birth and death, buying and selling, and no one knows the time of the end. What really happens in the formation of hope in the New Testament community is that the Christians now live in a "time between the times," having received the new reality of grace yet having to look in patience and in expectation toward the consummation of God's rule.

Only when we recognize this new structure of hope can we grasp the meaning of the striking paradoxes in which the new life in the Spirit is described. Some of Paul's sentences are especially powerful as they fuse presence and promise. "All things are yours, . . . the world or life or death or the present or the future, all are yours; and you are Christ's; and Christ is God's" (1 Cor. 3:21-23). The climax of the great passage in Romans 8, which begins with the whole creation groaning and travailing in pain, and the blunt assertion that we are saved in hope, concludes with the theme of absolute assurance: "Neither death, nor life, . . . nor anything else . . . will be able to separate us from the love of God. . . ." (Rom. 8:38-39). The content of the future is determined by the love of God. The form of the future is largely hidden; but it will be determined by the meeting of God's grace with the human condition.

The Meaning of the Resurrection

We have characterized the new relationship of presence and promise brought about by God's action in Jesus Christ. We have so far made no special reference to the resurrection, because we have been trying to see the new structure of hope as it emerges. But we must now see

the relationship of this new structure to the resurrection of Jesus and
to the doctrine of resurrection that arose in the Christian church.

There can be no question but that the sign of the resurrection was
the climax of the transforming history of grace through Jesus. His
resurrection became for the Christian community the form and ground
of hope for the overcoming of death. The resurrection of the body
becomes the door to the life everlasting in the Christian creed, although
in most of the apocalyptic program resurrection is also the prelude to
judgment and therefore is no guarantee of life everlasting in God.

What needs to be stressed in relation to our theme is that the resurrection of Jesus was not only a sign of God's present and future victory
over death; it was also the sign of God's victory over sin. Participation
in the resurrection is something offered to the believer who in faith
knows God's justifying grace. Jürgen Moltmann has treated the resurrection solely as a promise for the future.[2] This simply does not do
justice to either Paul's or John's interpretation of it. Paul's interpretation
of resurrection is filled with reference to the new life into which we
have already been raised with Christ. The passage in Romans 6, in
which Paul affirms that God has raised Christ from the dead so that
we might walk in newness of life, contains a futuristic element. But the
whole plea of the passage is for Christians to "consider themselves dead
to sin and alive to God" as a present reality. In Colossians Paul is quite
explicit: "If then you have been raised with Christ, seek the things that
are above. . . . You have died, and your life is hid with Christ in God."
There is a future hope in this new existence: "When Christ who is our
life appears, then you also will appear with him in glory" (Col. 3:1-4).

Thus the resurrection of Jesus opens the way to a new experience of
life and death in this flesh and in this history. We live in a new time
determined by God's victory that is both present and future. This new
structure of life in Christ with its hope gives its special character to the
life of the new community. It is life with assurance, "possessing all
things," and yet still life in this body with its aging, subject to accident
and death. It is sinful life in a tragic world where the principalities and
powers have been defeated yet remain threats.

We can enter into the faith and spirit of the New Testament community only as we ask our own questions about hope. There are at least
three major issues faith must meet.

The first is death itself. Some of the earliest Christian believers thought
they would not die before the Lord returned. Paul wrote the first letter
to the Thessalonians specifically to meet this question. Death remains
with its relentlessness, its forms of suffering, its seeming annihilation

of the person. We shall have more to say about the modern experience of death a little further along, but in spite of all techniques for prolongation of life and all ways of trying to keep death from threatening the meaning of life, we still understand what Paul means by saying death is the last enemy.

The second major issue concerns the haunting knowledge of the injustices of this life. There is the fate of individuals whose lives are twisted, thwarted, cast aside through no fault of their own. And there are the great moral wrongs: one person's injustice to another, the slaughtering of the innocents, the fatness of exploiters and tyrants, the complacence of the satisfied. Jesus' declaration that the meek shall inherit the earth is eschatological. In history, inheritance is often related to power and ruthlessness. Nikolai Berdyaev points out that the arrival of an ultimate, just state still leaves unresolved the justification of the suffering of those whose earthly lives have been shattered along the way.

Finally, there is an issue that theology has not yet fully faced: the mystery of the unfulfilled life of the spirit. Multitudes of creatures, despite God's will to save them, live and die without ever encountering the reality of love in any form in which it can be grasped.

In some sense this may be the universal condition. What right have we to say that we have seen the meaning of life? We cannot simply moralize about this. We have no guarantee we will not waste such vision as we have. What shall we say to the loss of the redeemable? Jesus weeps over Jerusalem, the human condition. In what sense is any lost generation redeemable?

Love and Hope: A Structural Analysis

Eschatology requires a certain indirectness in our attempts to understand. The eschatological symbols do not lend themselves to literal interpretation. We are seeking an inner tendency in the character of love as it looks into the future and wrestles with actuality. Let us try therefore to identify certain structural principles for understanding the relation of love and hope that begin to emerge from our analysis of the relation of presence and promise in the Bible. We have already seen in our phenomenological study of love[3] that it involves freedom. Love seeks communion with the other, but on terms of the other's freedom to be. This implies that to love is always to enter a history that has an undetermined outcome, and to know the risk of unknown elements. Love is essentially a venture in discovery. It has a prospective aspect.

We can now identify three major aspects of the relation of love and hope that receive decisive expression in the Bible.

First, to love is to participate in the creative freedom of God and the creatures. Therefore, to love is to be open to a future that is not known. The assurance that nothing can separate us from the love of God is not a prediction of future events but an orientation toward them, whatever they may be. Love knows the acceptance of risk, the risk of the creatures, and the risk God takes in granting us freedom. In love we do not ask to escape the risks, pains, and tragedies of existence. We live amid them, willing the new good to come in spite of or through them. Alfred North Whitehead said, "Religion is not a research after comfort."[4] Neither is love.

Second, love affirms and accepts judgment. We have recognized how the theme of judgment runs through the New Testament eschatologies. Jesus says, "Temptations to sin are sure to come, but woe to him by whom they come" (Luke 17:1). The Revelation of John sees the judgment of God cutting between the faithful and the unfaithful. "Nothing unclean shall enter [the new city] nor any one who practices abomination or falsehood, but only those who are written in the Lamb's book of life" (Rev. 21:27).

There are at least three reasons why theologies of many different types have tended to bypass the theme of judgment in speaking of the last things. The first is that many New Testament passages have a universalist tendency and seem to point to a complete overcoming of all evil. Second, there is a justified revulsion against the pathological use of the doctrine of eternal punishment to condemn to an eternity of suffering those who offend our sense of decency. Against all such moralizing in history, Christ will continue to seek out the lost for eternity. Thirdly, there is a tendency to individualism in traditional doctrines of the separation of the saved and the lost. We are lost and saved together, as members of the human race and as members of Christ's body. The doctrine of individual judgment must not obscure the solidarity of humankind. But this leaves us with the necessity of considering what we mean by judgment; it does not eliminate judgment from the encounter with God.

Love is involved in both immediate and ultimate judgment in two ways.

First, it is in the light of love that evil is judged to be evil. This is the basis for the relating of all Christian hope to present ethical decision. There is a link between the content of our hope for a new heaven and a new earth and present decisions in history. The link is our experience that whatever blocks our growth in love is evil. Whatever serves that growth, no matter its form or character, is good. Ultimate judgment does not set aside the need for proximate judgment upon social orders, upon individual acts, upon modes of life in this history. Injustice is always evil in the eyes of love.

That is why I suggest that Moltmann's use of the logic of contradiction as the basis of his interpretation of the meaning of the resurrection and Christian hope produces an insoluble problem in his theology. If the new for which we hope is the sheer contradiction of the present, there is no basis for choosing one way rather than another in politics, economics, or any other sphere of life. But Moltmann finds he must return to such terms as "human dignity and freedom."[5] These good things are surely not the exclusive possession of Christians. And if they are to be affirmed in whatever way in present history, then there is a positive continuity between present human action and the ultimate hope, however radical that final hope may be. Moltmann's assertion that "it is not human activity that makes the future" surely drains both present and future history of all meaning.[6]

There is a second issue in which love is related to judgment: Love constitutes the criterion of our hopes. Hope can be just as distorted by sinful self-centeredness as any other human expression. Our earthly hopes have an inevitable tinge of self-centeredness. We see the world in terms that gratify us individually and collectively. Sin enters in so easily. We comfort ourselves in the present enjoyment of privilege by hoping that one day justice will be done. We dwell in sentimental illusions about the future as a means of refusing to face the present. The very insistence on the glory of hope can be an escape from confession about the truth of the past and present. In Christian faith Kant's question, "What may we hope for?" needs to become also the question, "What ought we to hope for?" The only answer in faith to that question is, "What love requires," nothing more nor less. So love is greater than hope because love judges the forms of hope.

Third and most difficult concerning the relation of love and hope is the question of whether love must affirm a final and absolute victory in order to claim to be the meaning of life. This is the final issue for a Christian eschatology, and while the Bible leaves open the question of a universal salvation, it does seem to affirm in faith an absolute finality in the victory of God.

We have received a partial answer to our question in the New Testament view that to love God and one's neighbor is to participate in eternal life. The person who believes has eternal life. It is characteristic of love, of both human loves and the gospel's *agape* love, to be grounded in an ultimate and indestructible goodness. God is eternal. God's life goes on in loving creativity forever. To grow in love is to share in eternal life, and nothing can separate us from it. There is an abiding in eternity that is the destiny of love. This insight, of which the Platonists and the Romantics like Goethe have made so much, is valid for human love, and it has its New Testament counterpart, especially in the teachings of Paul and of the Fourth Gospel.

In process thought participation in the eternal life of God in every moment is not a detemporalizing of history. This is so partly because every pulsation of existence *is* a history. In each moment every entity lays hold of a possibility and moves toward some kind of resolution between its past determination and a new potential. In our human experience this future is not only the immediate future, but also the long future as structured in imagination yet always relevant to the present. Process theology also avoids the detemporalizing of history, because the eternal life of God is itself a history. To believe in the living God is to know our lives as joined with God's ongoing life.

That is why Christian faith cherishes every authentic growth in love. It is important not only for this life within the horizon of earthly history but important forever in God. Alfred North Whitehead speaks of the unfading importance of our experiences that perish and yet live forevermore. Every human action contributes to the future, its actuality, its limitations, and its self-valuation to be judged by the Supreme Valuer.

Yet with the discovery of the eternal dimension in the life of love there remains the final question of whether love leads to knowledge of an absolute fulfillment. Does love require such fulfillment? It is true that the New Testament in many places envisions a final triumph of God over everything standing in the way of the Kingdom. Is this perhaps an aspect of the absolutist doctrine in which God disposes of the creatures, as Whitehead says? Or is this something built into the nature of love itself; does love have its own secret hold on absolute victory?

We cannot speak of a resolution of this question on the basis of our knowledge. If we say it is a matter of faith, we still have to say what the content of faith is concerning the end. There seem to be two possibilities.

One is that faith in God requires an absolute assertion about the end. In faith we deny any ultimate loss and tragic element in history as God sees it. "Faith is the victory . . . that overcomes the world,"[7] in the sense that in faith we believe that in God all things are made right forever.

The other possibility is to remain faithful to the limits of our sight and to discover that love can accept life as having meaning, experiencing

victory over evil, and remaining always hopeful without knowing or
having to know that everything is finally transformed into good. In this
perspective we see no reason why God should not go on creating new
worlds forever, with new risks, new possibilities, new attainments. God's
love will never be vanquished and God's work will never be finished.
God's creativity will never cease. The importance of every achievement
of free creatures will never diminish. Indeed, it will always be further
enhanced because it contributes to new histories that pose issues and
decisions of significance to God.

In this mode of thinking of the end, there is acceptance of an element
of adventure, of not-knowing, within love itself. We surrender the absolute security of a final disposal of all evil for the continued risk and
creativity of a living movement in which love brings new life into being
without absolute guarantees, but with the assurance that nothing has
meaning outside of the abiding and creative love of God.

Life after Death

From within the second of these perspectives we turn to two specific
questions: life after death, and the progress of the Kingdom of God in
history.

Victory over death is a major theme of the gospel. What kind of
victory? The conception of "personal immortality" has usually become
an integral part of the Christian witness. The resurrection of the body
and the life everlasting are affirmed in the ecumenical creeds. When we
face death the question of whether this means the end of personal
existence presses upon us. Love affirms the personal worth in the unique
life of every individual. Miguel de Unamuno passionately argued that
love inevitably demands the continuance of life as this conscious personal
existence beyond death. He held that to believe in immortality in this
concrete sense is one with belief in God.[8] One of the distinctive aspects
of Christian faith is its assertion that the individual person is fulfilled
in salvation, not annihilated or absorbed into absolute unity.

Yet must we not at the same time do justice to the restriction that
comes from love itself: that we do not make the terms upon which such
fulfillment is achieved? It is God who measures and confirms what love
requires. To die within the covenant of love is to die knowing that
nothing can separate us from the love of God. It is to die giving life
up in trust to the One who binds all life together in ongoing creativity.
It is to die not knowing the form that the loving affirmation of life may
take.

There is much we do not know about death and its service to life. Human response in the face of death has many possible forms. We should not put them into a few stereotyped categories. Not all depends upon a consciously held picture of the future of personal existence. What then would be the necessary conditions of a meaningful faith in immortality that respects the limits of our knowledge and in which the spirit of love entrusts the whole of life to God? There would seem to be four requirements:

First, life after death must be a transformation of the form of this life. Purely naturalistic views of existence beyond death, which are simply extensions or reproductions of earthly life, do nothing to relieve the mystery and the threat of death. The results so far of claims to communication with the dead are thin in content and unsatisfying. Continued existence is not eternal life, however interesting and gratifying it might be to know that there is some such experience. Death marks a boundary between two modes of existence. Life beyond this present existence must surely be life in a new mode. Paul transformed the doctrine of resurrection by declaring that it is not this body that is raised but a "spiritual body." Thus, he keeps the unity of the person but provides a symbol that transcends earthly experience.

Second, to believe in immortality is to believe in an enduring significance to the actions of this life. Whatever worth those actions have continue in their significance for all subsequent action. This is the assertion that our labor is not in vain in the Lord (cf. 1 Cor. 15:14ff). To love is to treasure the uniqueness of each person and the irreplaceable worth of each personal relationship for others and for God.

What lies beyond our sight is the mode in which God treasures, uses, affirms, and enjoys each individual existence. We know that God does these things, for that is what love does. We do not know the form in which we are present to God. There are many possibilities. Even to state them takes us beyond what we can literally imagine. Creative memory preserves individuality and transforms it into new experience, and God's memory is supremely vivid and creative. Some theories of immortality have suggested that the person may acquire a new body. Certainly the spirit is not completely bound to this body even in our earthly existence. It can defy this body's needs, within limits. It is not beyond the range of possibility that there might be another structure with which the spirit involves itself. These theories are mentioned not to argue for their validity, but to suggest that the mode of personal survival could take many possible forms. Here also love has given rise to many forms of hope, and we need not decide between them.

Contemplation of immortality does not in itself remove grief and loss in the face of death. There are those who long for death, and perhaps those who long for oblivion. For the most part, however, death means real loss. We are bereft. This is part of the experience of human love. We try to preserve life, and usually we try to prolong it regardless of our view of immortality. Jesus' death was not an incident in an unruffled progress from this life to another. It was his sharing in the rent that death brings to human existence. He bore the shock and pain of losing his life. Surely, this is where his death touches us. And that is why the laying down of life is an ultimate test of love.

The third requirement of a loving hope beyond death is that we accept God's judgment upon all life. In the Bible, resurrection is usually the prelude to judgment. This is part of the seriousness of death. It marks the boundary of our effort in this life. It defines the scope of whatever value we have seen, and it sets a final stamp upon our failure. Process doctrine holds there is judgment in every moment. Each pulsation of life and each human decision achieves its boundary, its objective definition, in the sight of God and in relation to others. To accept judgment in love is to trust in a loving judgment. What our life is defined to be is finally for God's evaluation, not ours. What God values, and how the fragments of this life can be woven into a significant future, is far beyond our sight. That is why the art of loving is to love and let go without demanding perfection of ourselves or the universe. Jonathan Edwards's willingness to be "damned for the glory of God" is an authentic expression of the love of God.

Finally, love means openness to the future. It is expectancy and venture. It is an interesting question whether, if we really love life, we can ever will its complete cessation. We can will the cessation of life on this earth. We are beginning to think in a mature way concerning the deliberate ending of this life when age or disease has made its prolongation intolerable. But can we will the extinction of our self-conscious being?

Some theologians, such as Paul Tillich, have denied that belief in conscious personal existence after death is part of their Christian conviction. Others, like Unamuno, have made it a cardinal article of faith. The position we take here would stand as a third alternative to Tillich's and Unamuno's views. With Unamuno, we acknowledge love's craving for life, and we may hold conscious personal life after death as an authentic hope. There is no convincing reason for denying its possibility, and the hope need not be seen as evidence of a self-centered demand on God. It can be simply an affirmation of the will to glorify God and to enjoy God forever: an expression of the will to belong, not the will to possess.

Yet with Tillich we refuse to demand only one form of our participation in eternal life. Resurrection is a symbol of victory, and especially of the fact that the victory over death is won by God, not us. There are numerous symbols within which life with God may be affirmed and even in some sense imagined: eternal rest, continuing celebration, purgation and renewal, creative growth, communion, memory that recreates hope and is open to the infinite future with God. When death is met with love there is always an element of hope, not only for the overcoming of death but for a new depth of understanding of both hope and love. We hope for the disclosure of greater hope. After all, as Paul says, along with faith and love, hope abides.

Two Cities in History

What then is our expectation for human history? In our revolutionary age the hope for peace and justice has been asserted as the foundation of the Christian response to life. The biblical eschatology, with all its emphasis on the end, never disparages the hope that human life here and now can be healed of its diseases and disorders and can enter the community of life abundant. Forms of utopianism have again become powerful, sometimes in new communities of intimate loving association, and again in revolutionary movements that work for the end of tyranny, war, and injustice.

This new optimism, for all its prophetic fervor, raises the perennial questions of the limits of human effort, the persistence of the tragic side of human experience, and the illusory character of utopian hopes projected as ideologies of particular groups rather than as realistic estimates of possibility. We seem to have to learn both to reconstruct the whole of human life, in the faith that the Kingdom of God makes the ultimate revolution possible, and at the same time to "ride out" the storms of history, be prepared to face new problems when old ones are solved, and to deal with a human condition that is less than perfect no matter how many wrongs are righted.

Process theologians have never been simple philosophers of progress, but they have all had a progressive element of radical hope for human society. We cannot conclude for any one philosophy of good and evil in history on the basis of our doctrine of love. Our position is that the spirit of love always creates new forms of both hope and love in history.

Love sustains hope and leaves the question of what we ought to hope for subject to life, adventure, and the experience of history.

What we can propose in the light of our doctrine of love is an image for the understanding of human life in history in relation to the Kingdom. This is the image of history as the confluence of two cities: the City of Man and the City of God. This is St. Augustine's contribution to Christian thought. What I propose here is a variation on Augustine's theme.

Augustine defines the two cities by the loves that govern them. The City of God is determined by the *agape* love of God and neighbor; the City of Man by self-centered love that has the mark of sin upon it. This distinction must be maintained in some way in any Christian theology of history. But there is a certain difficulty in using it as the pattern for grasping the interplay of God's action and our response in history. Augustine's distinction, unless very carefully handled, tends to suggest that all human earthly efforts are determined only by sin. He allows for the use of secular orders, but does he sufficiently recognize that they may be forms for the expression of genuine love? As is well known, Augustine came close to identifying the church with the City of God. We are in need of another image of two cities based on a similar perspective, one that will do justice to the strange mixture of love, power, and justice in history as we recognize God's love at work among all the others.

I propose to define the two cities; that is, two communities within which human life is lived. First is the City of Man, which is the form of human life guided by the earthly loves and all the human needs understood within human categories, with attention fixed on the possibilities of human effort within the structure of human societies and civilizations. The second is the City of God, the Spiritual Community. It is the company of people in history who in some way, not necessarily in religious forms, have discovered the love of God at work and who see all human effort in relation to the divine purpose. It is roughly the difference between human life viewed and lived *sub specie humanitatis,* without Christ at the center; and life viewed *sub specie eternitatis,* with Christ as the bearer of the new *humanitas* that God wills and sustains in time, now and forever.

This is an attempt to give the City of Man its due as the scene of vitalities, creativity, work and play, culture-building and -destroying. In the City of Man the contest of life with life is ineluctable, and it goes on amid the search for structures of mutuality and ordered peace. The clash of ideas and values constitutes the stuff of human history. It is the scene of our search for what we want and who we are. This is not to say that in the work and clash of life we are nothing but self-centered. Generosity, self-forgetfulness, sacrifices for justice all belong to each of us as persons. The enjoyment of laughter and of the absurdities of existence is as essential to the abundant life as are religious ritual and solemnity. In the City of God everything in the City of Man that contributes to the release of human powers, and everything except the willful hurt of life, is accepted. But in the Spiritual Community all human values are seen in the light of the ultimate claim of self-giving, forgiving, redemptive love. This light transfigures the human loves, judges them, and, insofar as they are parochial, saves them from the emptiness that comes with frustrated life.

The City of Man lives by the human spirit with its creativity and freedom; yet it must give a large place to law, to the forms of coerced order, and to the institutions that give shape to human culture. Its institutions can become themselves the great Disorder, the source of their own self-destruction. Yet we cannot live without structures, as Paul and Augustine saw. In the City of God, the Spiritual Community freely allows the Spirit itself to set its boundaries. (This is one reason we cannot identify the church with the City of God, for the church must develop legalistic institutional structures.) The Spiritual Community does not reject law, but it lives from another source. It refuses to be bound by the prescribed necessities. It respects public order but knows that the order is never sufficient.

Yet those within the Spiritual Community are not warranted in feeling superior over those who struggle with the necessities of law and politics. An able black leader of a responsible political organization was once asked to comment upon the leadership of a distinguished politician who figured prominently in the discussion about racial justice. Someone asked him, "But don't you think candidate X's heart is right on the racial question? Doesn't he want to do the right things?" The wise leader replied: "When I judge a politician I am not concerned to look into his 'heart of hearts.' I want to know how he responds to political pressure." We live in two cities, and it is this fact that gives its tension and ultimate perspective to the Christian life in history.

In the City of Man the mark of passage is upon all things. All flesh is as grass. All cultural achievements finally disappear. The pyramids crumble, the masterpiece fades. Perhaps the earth itself can no longer sustain life. There is a heroism in people as they accept the passage and yet shore up their hope in the face of it in art, prayer, and liturgy. Stoic courage, naturalistic joy, proud defiance are human attributes. They reflect human greatness. Some even see *thanatos* conquered by *eros*. It is a utopian vision but a meaningful way to deal with life and death. In the City of God this passage is known and accepted. We have no continuing city in this life, but the City of God is infused with the knowledge of eternity. To live in the light of the eternal love of God is to accept the passage and transcend it. For faith, "the excellent becomes the permanent."[9] This is why the structure of the Christian liturgy is not only expectation but also the acknowledgment of the love that binds memory and hope together and celebrates the presence of Christ.

The City of Man harbors an internal tension about knowledge. Human beings are knowers. One of the triumphs of human culture is the pushing back of error and superstition through the growth of science and the achievement of critical intelligence. Yet our knowledge is fragmentary and riddled with ideology. In the City of Man we begin to learn our limits as well as to think of our achievements. But as human beings we seek to know everything.

In the City of God there is an analogous problem concerning knowledge. We enter the City of God through the Truth that has been disclosed in Jesus Christ. In him all truth coheres, so in the City of God our knowing is fed by all human discovery. Both cities are continually enriched by the insight that comes through the great minds and spirits: Gautama, Plato, Kierkegaard, Marx, Freud, Einstein. All illuminate the ultimate questions. Yet in the City of God we still see through a glass darkly. Any claim to infallible knowledge turns against itself. The progress of the spirit involves a deepening of humility about our knowledge. Mystery and meaning live in dynamic interplay. So, the two cities can understand one another and mutually criticize one another in the search for Truth.

Finally, we must consider the ultimate structure of sin and grace as it bears upon the two cities. In St. Augustine's doctrine we must assign the earthly city to the realm of sin, for it knows only a self-centered love. But there is danger in this. We have to see God at work in both cities and in their mutual involvement. Grace is present in secular forms and in surprising modes in all life. As Reinhold Niebuhr has reminded us, a hidden Christ operated in history.[10] And the City of God still must reckon with the presence of sin. Our highest aspirations are perverted by pride; our lives are bound up in the solidarity of the human family so that nothing that potentially hurts or destroys human life is alien to us even within the life of grace. That is why one mark of the reality of the presence of the Holy Spirit is awareness of the necessity of forgiveness.

The boundaries of the two cities are not for us to draw. Our image is but an instrument for trying to grasp something of the interweaving of struggle and salvation, delight and destruction, joy and hope, in human existence when lived under the sign of the cross and resurrection.

We can readily see that this view of history as two cities leaves open many questions about what is possible and about the form of Christian hope, whether it is universalist or whether we finally acknowledge a tragic element not only in human history but also in the life of God.

We cannot know the limits of what God may do with the wreckage of history, the lost opportunities, the bitter injustices that thwart the lives of multitudes, the ignorance, error, and prideful illusions of men and women. We know that all this is received by God in an absolute and transfiguring love. God's judgment upon it all is surely far different from ours. We can say that universal salvation is the inner yearning of love. There is nothing outside God's care. There is nothing too good to hope for. But to will the universal saving of every life, every occasion, every possibility, is not the same thing as achieving it. Until we learn that to will the complete victory of love is not to know that victory, and that we can continue to love without knowing it, we have scarcely begun to learn the depths of courage and hope that belong to the adventure of love in freedom.

Notes

Editor's Preface

1. A term used in John B. Cobb, Jr., and David Ray Griffin, *Process Theology: An Introductory Exposition* (Philadelphia: Westminster, 1976), 178.

Chapter 1. Faces of the Demonic

(*Source:* Previously unpublished material from Daniel Day Williams's Armstrong lectures, delivered October 9, 1973, at Kalamazoo College, Kalamazoo, Michigan.)

1. Two articles published in this period reflect Tillich's view. One, "The Kingdom of God in History," gave its title to a collection of essays, published in Chicago by Willett Clark & Co. in 1938. The other, "Freedom in the Period of Transformation," appears in *Freedom: Its Meaning,* ed. Ruth Wanda Anshen (New York: Harcourt Brace, 1940). [Ed.]

2. Reviewer of Thomas McGuane's *Ninety-Two in the Shade,* in *New York Times Book Review,* 29 July 1973, 1.

3. Paul Tillich, *The Interpretation of History,* trans. N. A. Rasetzki and E. L. Talmey (New York: Scribner, 1936).

4. Ernst Bloch, *Man on His Own* (New York: Herder & Herder, 1970), 224.

5. Tillich, *Interpretation of History* (New York, Scribner, 1936), 122.

6. Ibid.

7. Alfred Weber, *Farewell to European History: The Conquest of Nihilism* (London: K. Paul, Trench, Trubner and Co., 1947), 224.

8. Eugene Bianchi, "Pigskin Piety," in *Christianity and Crisis,* vol. 32, no. 2, 21 February 1972.

91

9. J. Glenn Gray, *The Warriors* (New York: Harper & Row, 1967), 51.

10. Paul Tillich, *Love, Power, and Justice* (London: Oxford University Press, 1954).

11. Rollo May, *Power and Innocence* (New York: Norton, 1972), 23.

12. Christopher Lehmann-Haupt, reviewing *Letters to Felice,* eds. Erich Heller and Juergen Born; trans. James Stern and Elizabeth Duckworth (New York: Schocken, 1973), in the *New York Times,* 25 September 1973.

Chapter 2. Breaking the
Demonic Power

(*Source:* Previously unpublished material from Daniel Day Williams's Armstrong lectures, delivered October 10, 1973, at Kalamazoo College, Kalamazoo, Michigan.)

1. Robert Linder, *The Fifty-Minute Hour* (New York: Holt, Rinehart & Winston, 1961).

2. The Nixon administration (1969–1974). [Ed.]

3. No exact reference has been found, but cf. Paul Tillich, *Systematic Theology* (Chicago: Univ. of Chicago Press, vol. 1, 1951; vol. 2, 1957; vol. 3, 1963), esp. vol. 1, 222–27, and vol. 3, 173–82. Williams also refers to Tillich's book, *The Interpretation of History*; cf. previous chapter, note 3.

4. James A. Sanders, *Torah and Canon* (Philadelphia: Fortress Press, 1972).

5. Paul Tillich, *The Courage to Be* (New Haven, Conn.: Yale, 1952); cf. esp. chap. 6.

6. Bloch, *Man on His Own.*

7. Albert Camus, *The Plague* (New York: Knopf, 1964).

8. Ernst Bloch, *Das Prinzip Hoffnung* (Frankfurt: Suhrkamp, 1959).

9. Roland H. Bainton, *Here I Stand: A Life of Martin Luther* (New York: Abingdon-Cokesbury, 1950), 185.

10. Paul Ricoeur, *The Symbolism of Evil* (New York: Harper & Row, 1967), 156.

11. Dag Hammarskjöld, *Markings* (New York: Knopf, 1964).

12. Abraham Joshua Heschel, *Man's Quest for God* (New York: Scribner, 1954), 49–50.

13. George Orwell, *Nineteen Eighty-Four* (New York: Harcourt, Brace, 1949).

14. Samuel Beckett, *Endgame* (New York: Grove, 1958); *Molloy* (New York: Grove, 1955).

15. Edward Albee, *Who's Afraid of Virginia Woolf?* (New York: Atheneum, 1962).

16. Samuel Terrien, "Modern Painting and Theology," *Religion in Life* 38 (Summer 1969), 179.

17. Samuel Terrien, "Demons Also Believe," *The Christian Century* 87 (9 December 1970), 1486.

Chapter 3. War in Heaven

(*Source:* Previously unpublished material from Daniel Day Williams's Armstrong lectures, delivered October 11, 1973, at Kalamazoo College, Kalamazoo, Michigan.)

1. Gray, *The Warriors,* 242.
2. Albert Camus, "Create Dangerously," in *Resistance, Rebellion and Death* (New York: Knopf, 1961), 269, 272.
3. St. Augustine, *The City of God* (New York: Random House, 1950); see especially books XI and XII.
4. Ibid., book IX, 20, 298.
5. Alfred North Whitehead, *Science and the Modern World* (New York: Macmillan, 1960), 191.
6. John Milton, *Paradise Lost,* book XII, lines 569–71.

Chapter 4. Mystery and Hope

(*Source:* Article by Daniel Day Williams in *The Christian Century,* vol. 71, no. 5, February 3, 1954, 138–40, entitled "Hope and Mystery in the Christian Faith." Used by permission of The Christian Century Foundation.)

1. 1954 Assembly of the World Council of Churches, Evanston, Ill.; Williams was a delegate to this Assembly. [Ed.]
2. Williams further develops this thought in an unpublished manuscript entitled "Christological Coherence," available at the Center for Process Studies, Claremont, California. [Ed.]
3. A more extensive development of this thought is found in "Encounter in Christ: The Work of Forgiveness," one of four unpublished lectures given by Williams as part of the biennial Nathaniel W. Taylor Lectures in Theology at Yale in 1953. The general topic of the Taylor series was "The Guilt and Renewal of Man." The other three lectures were: "Encounter and Guilt: Man as Self-Destroyer," "The Way to Selfhood: A Christian Theory of Self-Acceptance," and "Property and Community: Conflict and Reconciliation in Society." [Ed.]
4. The phrase "liberal theologies" refers to that movement in American theology, perhaps best exemplified in the work of Walter Rauschenbush, which emphasized the gospel as a force for social change. Williams's analysis of this movement can be found in his books *The Andover Liberals, a Study in American Theology* (New York: King's Crown Press, 1941); *God's Grace and Man's Hope* (New York: Harper, 1949); and *What Present Day Theologians Are Thinking* (New York: Harper, 1952). [Ed.]
5. The reference here is to the theological program of biblical exegete Rudolf Bultmann. See his *The New Testament and Mythology,* ed. Shubert D. Ogden (Philadelphia: Fortress Press, 1984). [Ed.]
6. Hannah Arendt, *The Origins of Totalitarianism* (New York: Harcourt Brace, 1951), 419.

Chapter 5. Tragedy and Hope

(*Source:* The Oreon E. Scott Lectures at Christian Theological Seminary in Indianapolis, given by Williams Feb. 24-28, 1962. The text of this lecture appeared as an article in *Encounter*, vol. 24, no. 1, 61-76. Used by permission of *Encounter*, Christian Theological Seminary.)

1. Nathan A. Scott, Jr., ed., *The Tragic Vision and the Christian Faith* (New York: Association Press, 1957), 53, quoting from Karl Jaspers, *Tragedy Is Not Enough*.

2. Ibid., 12.

3. James Russell Lowell, "The Present Crisis," in *The Poetical Works of James Russell Lowell*, vol. I (Cambridge, Mass.: Riverside Press, 1904), 18.

4. Scott, *Tragic Vision*, x. Italics appear in the original.

5. Brooks Atkinson, "Critics at Large," *The New York Times*, 12 December 1961, 40.

6. This observation would seem to be particularly true of the antinuclear movement in the 1980s, and especially of its religious participants. [Ed.]

7. Albert Camus, *The Rebel*, trans. Anthony Bower (New York: Knopf, 1959), 303.

8. George Santayana, *Character and Opinion in the United States* (Garden City, N.Y.: Doubleday, 1956), 70.

9. Nels Ferré, *Evil and the Christian Faith* (New York: Harper Bros., 1947), chap. xii.

10. For more recent literature on this subject in the specific contexts of South Africa and Central America, see Alan Paton, *Ah, But Your Land Is Beautiful* (New York: Scribner, 1981); Robert Stone, *A Flag for Sunrise* (New York: Knopf, 1981); and Manlio Argueta, *One Day of Life*, trans. Bill Brow (New York: Vintage Books, 1983; originally published in El Salvador as *Un Dia en la Vida*, 1980). [Ed.]

11. Karl Barth, *The Humanity of God* (Richmond, Va.: John Knox Press, 1960), 61–62.

12. George Santayana, "Ultimate Religion" in *The Philosophy of Santayana* (New York: Scribner, 1936), 572–86; *Realms of Being* (New York: Scribner, 1942), 523.

13. Paul Tillich, *Systematic Theology*, vol. II (Chicago: Univ. of Chicago Press, 1957), 43.

14. Williams has argued that his view stands in marked contrast to the position of Wolfhart Pannenberg. See Williams's "Response to Wolfhart Pannenberg," 83–88, and his "Hope and the Future of Man: A Reflection," 142–46, in Ewart H. Cousins, ed., *Hope and the Future of Man* (Philadelphia: Fortress Press, 1972). [Ed.]

Chapter 6. Love, Death, and Hope

(*Source:* Previously unpublished material from the Daniel Day Williams papers at the Center for Process Studies, Claremont, California.)

1. For Williams's full treatment of this image, see *God's Grace and Man's Hope* (New York: Harper, 1949), chap. 5; reprinted as "Time, Progress and the Kingdom of God," in *Process Philosophy and Christian Thought*, ed. Delwin Brown (Indianapolis: Bobbs-Merrill, 1971), 441–63. [Ed.]

2. Jürgen Moltmann, *Theologie der Hoffnung* (Munich: Kaiser, 1964), 187–88.

3. Daniel Day Williams, *The Spirit and the Forms of Love* (New York: Harper & Row, 1968).

4. See above, chap 3, note 5.

5. Moltmann, *Theologie der Hoffnung*, 303–4.

6. Ibid., 196–97.

7. These words are from the chorus of an evangelical hymn written by John H. Yates (1837–1900) with music by the well-known nineteenth- century Christian musician Ira D. Sankey. The hymn tune is called "Sankey". This hymn has appeared as part of two recently published hymnals. It is hymn #256 in the *Baptist Hymnal* (Nashville, Tenn.: Southern Baptist Convention Press, 1956) and is hymn #453 in *Hymns for the Living Church* (Carol Stream, Ill.: Hope Publishing Co., 1974).

8. Miguel de Unamuno, *The Tragic Sense of Life* (New York: Dover, 1954).

9. This sentence is from Jane Addams (1860–1935), American social worker and writer, founder of Hull House in Chicago, one of the first settlement houses in the U.S. Addams used these words as the title of a book, *The Excellent Becomes the Permanent* (New York: Macmillen, 1932).

10. See Reinhold Niebuhr, *The Nature and Destiny of Man* (New York: Scribner, 1941–1943).

Index

97